"The practical advice, insights and [...] Your Weight' will provide a valuable contribution to [...] entrepreneurship both in the UK and internationally. From setting a vision to achieving one's goals, John Potter's expert tips provide the definitive step-by-step guide to success for entrepreneurs and intrapreneurs alike. It is recommended reading for everyone on the journey towards personal and business success."

Helene Martin Gee, Founder, Pink Shoe Club, Chief Adviser, All-Party Parliamentary Group for Entrepreneurship

"John Potter is passionate about making people aware of the opportunities to run their own business. He is an avid promoter of all business models, which include franchising, mini-franchising and in particular sees network marketing as having great potential for the future of business. This book updates many of the ideas already written about in the well-known book by Napoleon Hill 'Think and Grow Rich' and will help anyone wanting to build a successful business."

Lynda Mills, Director General, UK Direct Selling Association

"John Potter has worked with me over a number of years on the many challenging issues entrepreneurs and micro businesses face. He has given me many useful insights, some of which are reflected in this book. Chairing an all-party parliamentary group on micro businesses I am sure this will be a useful tool in delivering success."

Anne Marie Morris MP, chair APPG Micro Businesses and Member of Parliament for Newton Abbot

"John Potter is a highly experienced and articulate business psychologist. He has considerable experience in training and developing negotiators and in leadership development. This book brings together many ideas from diverse sources including his own thinking and it will put many people on the right path towards becoming successful in both their business and their lives."

Jonathan O'Brien, CEO Positive Purchasing Limited

"John Potter is amongst a growing number of informed thinkers that recognise the power of being, or becoming an entrepreneur. He has been an avid promoter of the network marketing industry, as a way of allowing people to become involved in their own business, whilst at the same time having the support, training and mentoring, that they may well need to become successful. As more people recognise that working for themselves need not be any more risky than having a job, then this book will become a must read."

Bob Parker, Managing Director, Forever Living Products

"John Potter offers a great resource for anyone wishing to build their skills and reach their full potential. John Potter draws on his great experience in helping to develop leadership and business performance in the public and private sectors. He is passionate about employee engagement and has worked to develop leadership capability at all levels. His personal experience is evident in the approach he takes to building confidence and capability to release the talent of each person."

Janet Waters, Development Director, Growth Capability Limited

Punch above your weight!

How to succeed at whatever you want to do

John Potter

Thorogood Publishing Ltd

10-12 Rivington Street
London EC2A 3DU
Telephone: 020 7749 4748

Email: info@thorogoodpublishing.co.uk
Web: www.thorogoodpublishing.co.uk

A CIP catalogue record for this book is available
from the British Library.

Paperback ISBN: (10) 1854188658
(13) 9781854188656

Ebook ISBN: (10) 1854188666 (13) 9781854188663

Printed and bound in Great Britain by
Marston Book Services Limited, Oxfordshire

I dedicate this book

to

Anne

Jenny and Katie

Table of Contents

Chapter Six
Engaging with others...121

Chapter Seven
Influencing and persuasion skills...........................139

Chapter Eight

Skills for selling and negotiating ideas..........................159

Foreword

We live in a world where the entrepreneurial and enterprise mindset is becoming increasingly important for individuals to achieve success on a personal and organisational level. Gone are the days when the average person can aim to go to college or university, obtain qualifications and then be guaranteed a 'job for life'. Such a thing does not exist in our world today.

To cope with this ever-changing world of complexity and global connectedness, each one of us needs constantly to be developing our ability in terms of adding value to the context in which we operate and the work we undertake. This book addresses the important idea that in reality each one of us can be thought of as a business. In order to survive and be successful we each have a need to undertake personal marketing, sales activity in terms of our ideas and possible contributions, and to be productive in whatever form that takes. We also need to handle our finances competently and look after our own personal human resource, that is our well-being.

We are in effect suggesting that each of us needs to become more enterprising and entrepreneurial, whether we are in gainful employment in an organisation or setting our own course to develop our own business. What we do know is that to develop entrepreneurship we do not just need business knowledge and skills. We need coaching and mentoring input from those who have achieved success so that we can learn from them. Above all we need the right mindset, creativity and the ability to turn that creativity into marketable innovation in products and services. We need to become leaders and to develop our ability in areas related to both business skills and people skills. A term that has emerged recently is 'engagement', usually associated with 'employee engagement'. To be successful we need to be able to engage effectively with all the people who have an interest in what we do, not just the people who carry out work for us as employees or suppliers.

Every year thousands of books are written and published around the world on how to be successful in business and life in general. Some are academic, some philosophical, some technical in terms of business issues and some are both hard to read and to put into practice. This book is different in that it builds on a sound knowledge base of the principles of personal success and then presents some key issues from the growing knowledge base of neuroscience and applied psychology. In a world where technology is advancing at what seems to be an ever-increasing rate, there is a risk that our ability to interact with other humans does not keep pace with the requirement. We live in what is increasingly becoming a global village due to our ability to travel long distances by air in a relatively short time. This means that we now interact with a much wider range of national cultures than in the past and businesses are outsourcing to parts of the world where they believe they can take advantage of lower costs whilst not jeopardising quality. If the West is to survive and prosper, we have to add more value to justify our high labour costs, whether that value is created by entrepreneurs, micro-businesses, SMEs or employees working with large corporates and in the public and third sectors. Each one of us has the personal responsibility to develop our capabilities in all respects.

One fact that has always interested me is that self-employed people and small business owners tend to take much less time off work due to sickness. I do not believe it is simply that by not working they are losing money. Instead I suspect that the passion they have for their work enables them to overcome lethargy and the various challenges and pressure they meet along the way. One psychologist (I forget who!) said at one time that only one in 20 people is passionate about the work they undertake, particularly in large organisations. My hope is that this book will help aspiring individuals find their passion, create their vision for their future and build a strategy to bring that vision into reality.

As someone who is passionately interested in business, particularly entrepreneurship, micro business and SMEs, I believe that this book has the potential to change the way people think about how they work and what they are trying to achieve. This is particularly relevant to my role as Chairman of the APPG for Entrepreneurship.

I recommend you read this book as a way to help you set your personal direction and focus your efforts in a balanced way so that you live a life of well-being and achieve the success which you desire and which you deserve.

The Earl of Erroll

Chairman All Party Parliamentary Group for Entrepreneurship

House of Lords, Westminster, London

February 2015

Acknowledgements

Creating a book is a demanding task intellectually, emotionally and in practical terms of the time involved. The success of the process is greatly governed by the help that the author receives from a range of people with an interest in the book. The help I have received in the writing of this book has been second to none. There are so many individuals I need to acknowledge and thank that in some ways it is difficult to know where to start.

Firstly I have to acknowledge the writers and speakers who have influenced me over the years in terms of the sense I have tried to make of human beings and how they work together in terms of achieving success. Earl Nightingale, Napoleon Hill, Dale Carnegie, W Clement Stone, Maxwell Maltz, Bob Proctor, Robert Kiyosaki, Jack Canfield, Mark Victor Hansen, John Assaraf, Brian Tracy, David Rock, Jim Rohn, David Tony Robbins, Stephen Covey, Richard Bandler, John Grinder, Wallace D. Wattles, Zig Ziglar and countless others have given me some great ideas that have contributed to my own personal development. I have tried to acknowledge and attribute specific ideas where possible but, in case I have missed any, my thanks to the originator whoever you may be! Their books are listed in the Resources section at the end of this book.

Secondly I would like to thank the excellent management training and consultancy organisations with whom it has been a pleasure to work. The Chartered Institute of Personnel and Development, Pragmatica International Limited, Positive Purchasing Ltd, the former National School of Government, Growth Capability Ltd and the many business schools including Warwick Business School, Cass Business School, Exeter University Centre for Leadership Studies and Greenwich School of Management are just some of the names that come to mind. A particular mention should be made of the Defence Academy of the UK and the Joint Services Command and Staff College based in Shrivenham. For many years I have had the privilege of presenting material on leadership to their very high quality course members from around the world. That tradition continues with my involvement with the Joaan Bin Jassim Joint Command and Staff College in Qatar.

Thirdly there are the outstanding clients with whom it has be delightful to work both as an individual and as part of the work of some of the consultancy and training operations above. GKN Westland, The Wrigley Company Ltd, Sony, Philips, Mercedes Benz, the Kuwait Petroleum Corporation, OiLibya, and AWAL IT in Saudi Arabia are just some of the corporate clients I have enjoyed working with over the years. In terms of public sector there are many government organisations such as the Royal Navy and the Royal Air Force, the Ministry of Defence, Bramshill Police Staff College and the Scottish Police College with whom it has been a delight to work. My time at the Royal Military Academy Sandhurst introduced me to the study of leadership that has been a gift which I have treasured for the past three decades.

My favourite speaker bureau, DBA Speakers, has given me some wonderful speaking engagements including Covent Garden Theatre. I once had a goal to perform there as a musician but did not achieve it in that life!

Thank you to Katharine Bourke and Rhona Hope of the UK Government's Growth Accelerator programme for agreeing to review the draft. This programme has great potential for putting the UK back onto a sound business footing in the micro and SME business sectors. Frances Edmonds and James Jones of the highly prestigious D-Group in Mayfair, London have been a great source of inspiration and business support with their business networking events. And closer to home Debbie Hutchings, Human Resources Manager for Teignbridge District Council, has helped me relate some of the ideas in the book to local government and the public sector, particularly in the area of leadership through engagement.

My passion for entrepreneurship has been greatly fuelled by my involvement on the Advisory Board of the House of Lords All Party Parliamentary Group for Entrepreneurship and I thank Lord Merlin Erroll for the splendid foreword to this book.

Thank you also to the very kind friends and supporters who have inspired me to create this book. Some have read the draft and they have made some very valuable comments. Those individuals include Jonathan O'Brien of Positive Purchasing, Janet Waters of Growth Capability Ltd, Sara Fowler, Helene Martin Gee of the House of Lords APPGE, several contacts in the CIPD, Roland Daniels, Diana Boulter of DBA Speakers, Jacqui Grey of the Neuroscience Institute and Bob Parker of Forever Living Products. My particular thanks go to Anne Marie Morris, Member of Parliament for Newton Abbot, who fitted in reading the draft and giving me some fabulous feedback ideas. My thanks go to Ron Tanner of Live Action Media for his help and technical expertise in making the taster videos which can be found on youtube. My thanks also go to Paul Barclay for his perceptive illustrations. Paul is becoming an international star in his creative work.

My publishers Thorogood and Falconbury have been delightful to work with over the years in terms of delivering workshops and courses and it has been a wonderful experience to partner with them for the production of Punch Above Your Weight!

Finally my sincere love, devotion and thanks go to my better half Anne who literally saved my life during a particularly black period in my life when I needed to draw on all my knowledge of psychological and financial survival skills. The day her little green car drove into my life changed things for the better forever. Thank you so much for your support and comments on the draft of this book.

The author

John Potter is an experienced speaker, consultant and trainer who has worked with many cultures around the world as a leadership development specialist.

He started his career as an electronics engineer and focused on medical electronics and measuring the electrical signals given off by the human body. Subsequently he widened his work into the area of social psychology and completed his PhD on Leadership and Stress. He has worked with many corporate organisations and government departments as well as holding a number of professorial appointments in higher education.

He has co-authored three books on leadership and one on the psychology of terrorism. His training work has ranged from corporate executives and public sector leaders to salespeople, military personnel and hostage negotiators.

The illustrations by Paul Barclay

Paul Barclay is a world-class illustrator whose studio is in Dartmouth, Devon, England. He specialises in creating illustrations in the world of yachts and superyachts and works around the world with high-profile clients. For this book he has interpreted the theme of each chapter in a way that should be a constant reminder of the subject material.

His website is www.paulbarclaydesigns.com

Introduction

Success means different things to different people. We all want to be successful at something and have aspirations to be happy and to grow as people. The world economy is changing to the extent that no longer can we rely on having a 'job for life'. Even occupations which were, in the past, very secure are now experiencing unprecedented change. The aim of this book is to provide you with a toolkit to enable you to be successful in whatever you undertake and it will give you specific skills to bring your dreams and your personal vision of how you would like your future to be into reality.

Most of us underperform

Although this is a bold statement, which you may question, it is true that relatively few people are successful at creating a fulfilling lifestyle as well as creating great success in their career or their business. Success is not just about money or material goods, it is a much wider state related to state of mind, happiness, sense of fulfilment, physical health and feeling well-rewarded for the efforts we make in our job or business.

Most of us consistently underperform and set our goals and aspirations too low to avoid people ridiculing us if we do not achieve our aims. It has been said by many writers that only around one in twenty people is passionate about what they do for a living. Many people drift into careers due to parental pressure, and taking advantage of work opportunities instead of designing a lifestyle. This book will enable you to become that one in twenty by giving you the tools to find out what you really want to spend your time doing and to create that magical life-style you really want.

The human brain is an amazing organ and we are just starting to understand a little about how it works and how we can use our brains more effectively. Neuroscience is becoming a key subject in the development of the human race in that we are beginning to understand how our brains work and how to use them to our best advantage. In particular the ability to think effectively is going to be even more critical in the increasing level of complexity and interconnectedness we are seeing in the world today. By using some of the more profound and practical ideas from psychology, neuroscience and philosophy we can all work towards becoming more effective in achieving our goals and having a happy, fulfilled and successful life in whatever career, profession or lifestyle you desire.

Think of yourself as a business

The fact is that you can have anything you really set your heart on and, to prove this, I am going to get you to think of yourself as a business. Like any business, you have a marketing depart-ment, a sales department, a production department, an admin-istration department, a human resources department to take care of your well-being and a finance department. If a business failed to pay attention to any one of these areas, it would not be successful and so, right from the start, we are going to talk about work-life balance to ensure that all these areas are taken care of.

The real world operates according to a number of well-defined laws. Work against those and life is tough. Work with them and you will achieve what you set out to achieve. Everything you acquire is governed by these laws – relationships, career, money and health are all functions of whether you understand and apply those laws and the principles that create them. We seldom hear about these laws during our education which often tends to focus on just acquiring knowledge. However, knowledge on its own is not particularly useful. It is the application of that knowledge that is important and that is where the Laws of the Universe fit in. More of this later!

We need a true understanding of ourselves as well as academic and vocational knowledge. It is how we apply that knowledge and engage with others that is important. And this is true for all of us as we go through life in terms of our careers and our businesses. Most people spend more time planning their holidays than their career or their business life. Success in the fullest sense needs application and discipline.

The tip of the iceberg

Punch Above Your Weight! explores some key issues which will enable you to move forwards in terms of success at whatever you undertake. You will notice at the end of the book that there are some suggestions for further reading. Every book has been carefully chosen to enable you to explore the ideas introduced in each chapter which you feel are particularly useful for your own position. Most of the books are easy to read and practical, although I have included some more serious titles to enable you to dig as deeply as you wish into topics such as leadership, negotiation skills and personal performance. However, this book is not just about giving you knowledge. It is about you gaining insights to enable you to apply knowledge. You can plot your progress with the dashboard at the end of each chapter.

Gaining insights, not just knowledge

One of the most useful recent contributions from the world of neuroscience is the understanding of how we create and experience insights. Initially we identify a topic which challenges us. Instead of forcing ourselves to find a solution it is more useful, according to the neuroscientists, to relax and reflect calmly on the issue in order to put our brain into the right state by allowing it to make new neural connections. This tends to happen when we feel good about things rather than stressed about them. The skills of reframing and disciplining yourself to think of the potential advantages and good points of even the most difficult situation are vital. If we can put ourselves into a positive state, our brain experiences the production of neurotransmitters such as serotonin which seems to increase the conductivity of our neural networks. In simple terms, we put ourselves into the right mental state to come up with ideas. If we develop the ability to run our brain effectively, we will experience 'illumination' moments of insight where various neurotransmitters are released such as dopamine and serotonin. It is important to act on the insight as soon as possible because the motivation stage can be short-lived unless we do so. So when you are reading this book, reflect on the ideas and work at feeling good about things – no matter how bad they seem. Then take action!

So let us get started!

In the next chapter we are going to review some of the thoughts on personal and business success that have been created over the past decades. Some of the works of these individuals are mentioned in the Resources section at the back of the book to enable you to drill down more deeply into what each guru has to say about success. A common theme throughout the book is one of the most significant Laws of the Universe, namely the Law of Attraction. This law has been presented in many formats and there is a logical application to support its validity. We will explore the law and apply its principles throughout the book.

So to summarise how you can benefit from reading this book:

- Keep focused on your vision and set clear goals

- Manage your emotions and don't let them get in the way

- Do what is necessary to work daily towards your vision

- Consider others and see things through their eyes

- Work at feeling good because your brain will work more effectively

- Build on your strengths and find your passion in life

- Remember that you become what you think about

- Apply the Law of Cause and Effect. You create the causes so that you can reap the effects

- Get your fundamentals rights – family, relationships, sense of purpose and your finances

- Things take time to come into being – the Law of Gestation

- Develop your self-awareness and notice how you impact on others

- Remember you are unique and have the potential to become what you want to become and to achieve all you want to achieve

- Work with others and build on their strengths to enable them to become successful

- Enjoy the process you are about to go through!

Chapter One
Why this book?

"The will to win, the desire to succeed, the urge to reach your full potential...these are the keys that will unlock the door to personal excellence." **Confucius**

Understanding the purpose of this book

The subjects of personal success, business success and fulfilled living have a history going back to ancient times. However, in the 20th century, much has been written about the Laws of Success and what it takes to be successful. This book is intended to give you an insight into some of the ideas of a number of key writers on this subject and, at the end of the book, you will find a reading list in the Resources section which will enable you to extend your knowledge in whatever direction you choose. The point of this book is to short circuit the task of reading the many books on success and to distil the common thinking into one relatively compact volume which you can use as your personal template for success. A number of areas are covered which will enable you to move forwards in terms of success and, in doing so, give your vision and goals 'legs' by taking practical action. What is becoming abundantly clear is that success is not just about having a vision but of taking the necessary actions to bring that vision into reality. We must not underestimate the role of vision because a clear vision charged with emotion tends to set up filters in our perceptual processes to identify opportunities to move forwards towards our goals through engaging our reticular activating system, the selective perception process. There is more about this in Chapter Three. What matters, as the American motivational speaker Zig Ziglar suggested, is to plan for success, prepare for success and expect success. That process is what will set up the filters so that we become tuned into opportunities to move forward.

We need to learn to manage our thought processes effectively because it is becoming increasingly obvious that we become what we think about. Think of bad things and unconsciously you will tend to make those bad things happen. Think of good things and you will tend to engage your unconscious mind to make them happen. You have the choice. One of the results of research into neuroscience is that when we have positive thoughts, our brains operate more effectively due to the greater conductivity through the neural connections. In addition we produce the biochemistry of success with neurotransmitters such as serotonin and dopamine which seem to be contributors to feelings of well-being and happiness.

On the other hand, when we feel under pressure or stressed, our ability to be creative and generate ideas can be inhibited by cortisol, a stress hormone produced by the adrenal glands. Thus if we want to ensure that our brain works effectively, we need to focus on thoughts that make us feel good.

Gratitude and expectancy

It is helpful to think about gratitude and expectancy. We tend to focus on our problems much of the time and so put ourselves into a negative state, dampening down our creativity and our motivation. By thinking about all the things for which we are grateful such as where we live, our house, our family, our career and the other good parts of our life, we can shift ourselves into a very positive state. The other word we need to remember is 'expectancy'. We need to have a positive expectancy as we tend to create and become what we think about. A negative expectancy will close down our neural connections, we will feel bad and open the filters to ensure that what we do not want to happen actually does happen. It is all about the power of a positive vision of what you want to achieve and then taking the necessary actions to bring that vision into reality. An important point in this respect is to focus on the vision and the benefits you will experience from its creation rather than worrying about whether you are going to be successful. That worry will tend to reduce the effectiveness of your thought processes and thus work against you.

So who started thinking about how we can become more successful?

So let us now start to look at some of the writers through the past century on what it takes to be successful. It seems there is a core set of skills to ensure success and we can all develop those skills to become successful at whatever we want to do. The following are just some of the people who have made a great contribution to our understanding of what it takes to be successful. We will pull together the common themes and then set about helping you to use the ideas to develop some insights on how you can move forwards.

Wallace D. Wattles

One of the first notable writers was Wallace D. Wattles who proposed a number of Laws of the Universe which can help guide us in our efforts to achieve success. His approach was to suggest that it was not doing certain actions which make you successful but doing things in a certain way. He argued that we are all connected with the universe through an energy field and that human thought is energy. Focusing on something you wish to achieve impacts on the energy field, according to Wattles, and tends to result in what you are desiring coming to pass. He proposed several Laws of the Universe of which perhaps the most significant is the Law of Attraction. This formed the basis for the film The Secret, which inspired so many people to achieve their ambitions. The Law of Attraction proposes that thoughts are 'things' and that you create your own environment based on your predominant thoughts. Think of debt and you seem to acquire more debt. Think of illness and your health starts to suffer. Many world-class figures have identified this fact. For example Winston Churchill stated, "Your thinking creates your world."

We will look in more detail at these Laws later in this chapter. The fundamental argument is that everything in the universe is really energy. If you look at your hand with an electron microscope and increase the magnification you first see molecules, then atoms and then...energy. Wattles was way ahead of his time in talking about energy and today quantum physics supports his idea that we are all manifestations of energy. The Law of Transmutation suggests that energy cannot be created or destroyed, the Law of Attraction states that like attracts like and the Law of Cause and Effect means we have to take action if we want to create outstanding results and bring our vision into reality. These three Laws are very powerful and there are others as you can see if you read Wattles' book. We will explore some of their applications throughout this book.

Why don't we learn about the Laws of the Universe at school?

The problem is that we do not often receive any guidance on how to use them. Certainly the education system in schools, colleges and universities does not cover them, preferring instead to focus on teaching people content and knowledge in order to pass examinations and gain 'qualifications'. I have worked in a number of business schools as a professor, yet in none of them has the Law of Attraction ever been mentioned and, even worse, little teaching takes place on topics such as personal vision, goal setting, negotiation, selling skills and all the subjects we really need to be good at to survive and prosper in this increasingly changing and complex world. This book is going to correct that situation! We are going to work through the really important topics to give you a toolkit for success for you as a business person, whether you intend to create and run your own business or achieve great things in the corporate world or the public sector. The material is just as important for careers in the third sector of charities and also non-government organisations, the military and the police. It is a recipe for outstanding success in whatever line of work you decide to undertake.

Think and Grow Rich

Putting aside the 'energy' model and the Laws of the Universe for the time being, perhaps the most read book about success in life is *Think and Grow Rich*, written by Napoleon Hill. This book has inspired thousands of people during the 20th century, particularly those in sales and direct selling organisations. Hill suggested 13 principles of success, which reflect Wallace D Wattles' theory, and put them into more practical terms. According to Hill, the 13 key principles of success are based on the idea that thoughts are things:

1. Desire to be successful - you need passion!

2. Belief that you can be successful and the faith to persist

3. Auto-suggestion and affirmations to support your belief and maintain your focus

4. Gaining specialised knowledge in your chosen area

5. Creativity and imagination to create your vision

6. Organised planning, goal setting and progress monitoring

7. Effective decision making

8. Persistence and overcoming 'bumps in the road' along the way

9. Tapping into the Mastermind Group principle

10. Energy transmutation through focus and a positive mindset 'I can'

11. Enlisting your subconscious mind to work with you rather than in opposition

12. Making the best use of your brain using the principles of neuroscience which has recently shed great light on how our brains work

13. The sixth sense and enlisting the help of your intuition

Hill also talks about learning to overcome fear and those concerns which can hold us back. The fact is however that *Think and Grow Rich* was written many years ago in a very different world and skewed towards the American culture. Nevertheless it still makes a major contribution to our thinking about how to become successful, particularly in business.

Some months ago I produced a series of short videos on leadership with the help of several highly successful Chief Executives and Managing Directors. The most inspirational of these was the interview with Bob Parker, Managing Director of Forever Living, a highly successful company in the wellness industry. One of the first things Bob told me was how he had been inspired by Think and Grow Rich. It seems that book has been the foundation for the success of many people through the decades and is just as relevant today as when it was written. If we now add the input of neuroscience, modern psychology and neurolinguistic programming to Hill's thoughts, then we truly have a powerful toolkit to help create our personal success in today's world.

Zig Ziglar

Zig Ziglar was a very inspirational American speaker on motivation, selling skills and values-based living. He suggested the idea of the Stairway to Success in which he promoted the idea of personal success being based on sound foundation values of honesty, faith, love, loyalty, integrity, and that old-fashioned word 'character'. He emphasised the importance of self-image, good relationships, goals, a positive attitude, hard work, and desire in the journey towards success. He had many insightful sayings such as: "You can get everything you want if you help enough other people get what they want." This is a great insight for the business person. Ziglar pushed the issue of positive belief rather than just positive thinking and his basic approach, as we have already mentioned, is to plan for success, prepare for success and expect success. What you plant today you reap tomorrow and you can start today with what you have got, develop your ability and go wherever you want with your life, your career and your business. This emphasises the importance of positive belief and how our beliefs play a major part in shaping our behaviour. Positive belief is based on reasons why you can 'move mountains' whereas positive thinking is just based on hope.

Zig Ziglar emphasised the importance of self-discipline and planning. To help you move forward in this area, the performance planning tool which appears later in the book in Chapter Eleven will help you create that discipline and high level of productivity. As Ziglar once said, "Life is tough. When you are tough on yourself, life will be infinitely easier on you."

Jim Rohn

Jim Rohn was also a very successful motivational speaker, business philosopher and sales professional who rose from humble beginnings in the United States of America to be a world-class celebrity and ambassador for business. One of the major contributions he made was the idea of how to develop your business and work philosophy. The starting point is to understand some of the factors in your development and conditioning by the people with whom you grew up and the experiences you went through during life. This conditioning leads to the creation of your set of beliefs about yourself, your abilities, about the world in which you live and so on. The beliefs process the events you experience and create thoughts, feelings and behaviours about the event. This is the basic idea of cognitive behavioural psychology which has become very popular in the therapeutic context. Your beliefs determine how you respond to opportunities and threats and lead to the formation of your attitude with regards to the event and the actions you subsequently take. We will look at this idea in more detail in the next chapter.

Jim Rohn wrote a number of books and made many videos. One of his most useful books is *7 Strategies for Wealth and Happiness*, first published in 1985. While the book is orientated towards the American public, the ideas and strategies quoted do help us work towards creating our plan for success. His seven ideas were:

- Create your strategy – create your plan, your vision for the future and set goals

- Seek knowledge – develop that Growth Mindset we talk about in neuroscience

- Develop change skills – become a master in handling change at all levels

- Take control of your finances – this builds psychological security

- Manage your time effectively – this is the key to focus and adding value

- Network widely – develop relationships with positive people who will help you

- Create work-life balance – build exercise, relaxation and pleasure into your life as well as work

Earl Nightingale

Earl Nightingale has been perhaps the most enduring thinker and speaker on personal and business success. He was an accomplished broadcaster in the United States of America and subsequently internationally. Two of his major achievements were the audio programmes *The Strangest Secret and Lead the Field,* initially produced as long-playing vinyl records and available today as CDs, ideal for playing in the car on the way to work!

His *Strangest Secret* programme was based on the idea that we become what we think about. It is, however, *Lead the Field* which has inspired many people to achieve great things. His philosophy starts with the importance of what he calls the Magic Word – attitude. He emphasises that it is your attitude at the start of a task which, more than anything else, will bring about a successful outcome. Your attitude to others determines their attitudes towards you. People do not develop a great attitude when they achieve success. Instead they achieve the success because of their great attitude. Recent research at Harvard University suggests that 85% of the reason individuals are appointed to jobs is as a result of a positive attitude rather than technical ability. Other topics Nightingale addresses are goal setting, realising the potential in whatever work you are doing at the present time, your attitude to money and the importance of understanding what he calls the Miracle of Your Mind. Details of his audio programmes are given at the end of this book.

Are you reaching your potential?

So how do you feel you are doing in terms of becoming successful, however you define success? Are you doing the things necessary to help you reach your potential?

The fact is that most people only tap into a tiny fraction of their potential abilities and we are not really given any guidance on how to do this during our education in schools, colleges and universities. Modern approaches to psychology and neuroscience, the science of the brain, teach us that our potential is virtually unlimited, only held back by our belief system of what is possible. As we have already suggested in modern society, it is estimated that only about one in 20 individuals is passionate about the way they earn their living. A recent survey by the UK's Chartered Institute of Personnel and Development in the UK suggested that over 85% of employees would change their job and way of life if they felt it were possible. In an ideal world, people in the workplace should be exhilarated by their jobs, authentic and genuine in their working relationships, receptive to new ideas, emotionally involved in their work, proactive in terms of sorting out problems, good achievers and advocates of the organisation in which they work. It is within your power to become one of the 'one in 20'.

The problem is that most often they are not happy with their work and leave either due to frustration or disenchantment with their immediate manager or a sense of a lack of fairness in how they are being treated. The reasons why people actually leave organisations are interesting:

- Poor management and leadership and not trusting their boss

- Inability to use their core skills

- The work is boring or not stimulating

- Feeling unappreciated and not valued by the organisation

- A lack of personal development

- Frequent reorganisations

- Not feeling involved in core issues related to their job role

- Feeling that the job is 'time hungry' compared to the overall remuneration and benefits package they receive

Do you relate to any of those issues?

It is not surprising that so many people are thinking of starting their own business and becoming their own boss. The problem is that most people have never had any training or experience in running their own business and so find it extremely difficult. In Chapter Two we are going to look at the underlying issue of whether you really are suited to running your own operation or whether it would be more in keeping with your abilities to develop your knowledge, skills and attitudes as an employee. Not everyone is suited to becoming a self-employed entre-preneur but for those that hold the idea as part of their dream, great experiences await! This book will position you to be either a very successful entrepreneur or a top-class employee, sought after by many organisations because of your reputation.

So let us proceed!

Let us start by summing up some of the ideas in this chapter and then getting you to think through how you can apply them.

Summarising success

You should create your personal strategic plan and have a clear vision of where you want to be in, say, three to five years. Plan for success, prepare for success and expect success. This book will give you a toolkit for doing this work.

Focus your thinking on what you want to achieve, not what you want to avoid. The vision board idea mentioned in Chapter Three will help you with this process.

Set goals. Do so in the creative and scientific way outlined in Chapter Three and then link those goals to your vision board.

Work on developing your networking skills and associate with positive people who are already achieving success. This will motivate and inspire you to go the extra mile in your work.

Remember, life can be tough and it is important to develop resilience to cope with the setbacks which will invariably occur along the way. By setting goals effectively, such setbacks become simply 'pebbles on the beach' rather than brick walls in the way!

Development questions

- If you knew that you could not fail, what would you try to achieve?

- What are you most passionate about in your life?

- Where would you like to see yourself in five years' time?

- Which three motivational writers and speakers listed in the Resources section will you focus on by acquiring either their books or their CDs?

- What is your definition for success as it relates to your life?

- Have you created your 'gratitude list', that list of things for which you are truly grateful?

- Have you noticed examples of the Laws of the Universe at work, that is, the Law of Attraction, the Law of Cause and Effect and the Law of Transmutation?

- Do you understand that another Law, the Law of Gestation, means that things do not tend to happen instantly but they take time, just as nature takes time for plants to grow and for animals to develop before they are born?

- Can you identify any negative beliefs which you feel are holding you back?

- Taking each of those beliefs individually, what would it be more useful for you to believe?

Now please rate your progress for Chapter One and complete the first mini circle 1 on the Progress Dashboard.

Your progress dashboard

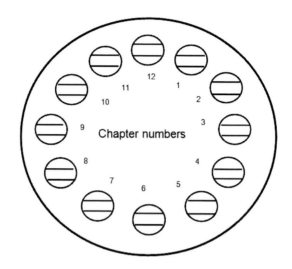

 I understand most of the ideas in this chapter and intend applying those which appeal to me

 I fully understand the ideas in this chapter and having made some progress in applying them

 I am fully committed to applying the ideas in this chapter and have made great progress and I am moving forwards with achieving my goals as I set new ones

Chapter Two
Understanding yourself

"Know yourself to improve yourself." **Auguste Comte**

One thing seems to stand out with people who are successful in whatever activity in which they involve themselves: they have self-awareness and a clear sense of their identity. This may not be a conscious awareness but they just know when things feel right and they take the appropriate action as they see it. There are many ways we can develop self-awareness including self-reflection, feedback from others, psychological tests and an awareness of what really excites and motivates us. One of the great tragedies of modern life is that people often pursue careers that seem to be appropriate whereas in reality their underlying potential is to do something else, perhaps something that does not meet the expectations of their parents, teachers, family members and peers. One of the keys to developing personal success, whatever your personal definition of the word, is to create your vision for the future and then identify your passion and your personal mission – find the activity that really excites you.

Life is about perception

Successful people tend not to think of their work as work but as the activity in which they really want to engage. What is work to us and what is play is a very personal definition and it all depends on our perception. I once interviewed a park gardener who, I felt, had possibly the most wonderful job in the world: working outside with nature, seeing the products of his work, and occasionally interacting with the public who complimented him on his efforts. I thought this job must be bliss, something I would do even if I did not get paid for it. When I suggested that he must feel lucky, he rebuked me in no uncertain terms and spoke very negatively about his job. He would rather have been at home in his shed building model railroad engines! Some weeks later, I was talking with a technician who made models of the company's products in an aircraft factory. Remembering my conversation with the gardener, I talked positively about how good his job must be in terms of creative satisfaction. He didn't see it that way. He was disappointed about the lack of care the salespeople took of his models at exhibitions. He went on to say that he would rather be at home tending his roses. So, what is work to one person can be a joyful self-fulfilling activity to another! It is all about perception.

The developmental flow of a person and what makes them tick

Programming and conditioning

Beliefs

Attitudes

Actions and behaviours

Results and outcomes

Lifestyle

Our early upbringing conditions us to view the world in certain ways. We are programmed by our parents, those around us and our teachers as well as the experiences we undergo. In an ideal world those conditioning and programming factors should develop our self-confidence, healthy positive beliefs, a sense of integrity and fairness and other qualities which will help us to work towards the goals and vision we wish to achieve. However, for many people, their conditioning has sowed the seeds of limitation, lack of confidence, poor self-image and what we will see later can be called 'poverty consciousness'. Remembering the Law of Attraction, which suggests we become what we think about, you can see how important it is that those conditioning factors are positive. The crucial issue in the developmental flow is the belief stage. Most people carry around with them negative beliefs which have been programmed into them by well-meaning but inappropriate role models. One of the first things we need to do if we want to move forwards is to identify those negative beliefs which are holding us back. We started this process in the questions at the end of Chapter One which asked you to identify any negative beliefs you have about yourself and your life which might be holding you back. A classic example of this is that many people have a negative belief about their ability as a public speaker, usually programmed in by a negative experience during their school days. To deal with this negative belief situation, we have to remember the Law of Gestation and accept that it will take a little time and reprogramming with both positive experiences and reminding ourselves of the belief that would be more helpful.

Let's look at the public speaking example. You currently have a negative belief: "I am no good at public speaking." This is not helpful! A more useful belief would be: "I am a confident professional person who is learning to become an excellent public speaker to whom people listen." That more useful positive belief can then be the foundation for an affirmation, something we will discuss later in this book. A word of warning. Do not try to simply substitute the belief: "I am an excellent speaker." Your unconscious knows the truth and you may well get into difficulty as a result of poor preparation due to the false sense of confidence you have induced. The positive element is to develop the belief that you are in the process of learning to be an excellent speaker. That way the door is open to your development and your unconscious cannot interfere.

And that is where we need to look at an important aspect of neuroscience, the distinction between having a Growth Mindset and a Fixed Mindset.

Developing your Growth Mindset

For some time we have tried to understand the mindsets that people tend to have particularly in the workplace. There are many differences in the way people tend to think about work.

More recently Daniel Pink, in his work on motivation and his book *Drive*, has focused on what really motivates people. Type X people tend to be motivated by extrinsic factors such as positive and negative reinforcement whilst Type I people tend to be motivated by intrinsic factors such as sense of purpose, mastery and autonomy. Both of these models on thinking and mindset seem to be sound intuitively. However, it is the developments in the world of neuroscience that have now given us the scientific evidence to support our concepts. Neuroscience has suggested the idea of the Growth Mindset which has the following characteristics:

- The belief that we are born to learn

- That we can change

- Making an effort is central to that change

- Feedback is helpful in terms of developing our ability to perform

- Stretch goals are good

- Other people's success is an opportunity to learn

Contrast this with the Fixed Mindset which many people still display:

- Our level of intelligence is something we are born with and cannot develop

- We cannot change much

- Effort does not help

- Feedback is dangerous

- Stretch goals are dangerous

- Other people's success is a problem

So the issue we need to consider as we move through our development journey is the extent to which we show a Growth Mindset. If your mindset is fixed, then you will find it difficult to move forwards towards your success.

See how you measure up on the following questionnaire.

Score each item out of 10 where 10 is total agreement, 0 is total disagreement.

1. Do you believe people are born to learn? _____

2. Everybody, including me, has the ability to change _____

3. We need to use the Law of Cause and Effect to make the efforts central to the changes we wish to make _____

4. I actively look for feedback as it is helpful in terms of developing my ability to perform _____

5. I thrive on stretch goals _____

6. I love it when others are successful as it is an opportunity to learn _____

7. Do you believe people are born with their level of ability or can it be improved? _____

8. It is difficult for people, me in particular, to create sustained change _____

9. Effort doesn't really make much difference in terms of results _____

10. I dislike feedback because it undermines my self-confidence _____

11. Stretch goals are bad because they cause pressure and stress_____

12. Other people's success is a problem to me _____

Hopefully you have answered the questions truthfully!

Total up your scores for 1 to 6. A score between 50 and 60 shows a strong Growth Mindset.

Total up your scores for 7 to 12. A score between 50 and 60 shows a strong Fixed Mindset.

Most people will tend to be in the middle areas and the point of this questionnaire is for you to identify the areas which will take you into a strong growth mindset and largely eliminate the fixed mindset.

Putting your Growth Mindset to work.

So what makes you tick? What is your WHY? What does success really mean to you – is it money, a great business, health, great relationships, recognition or any of the other factors which so often arise when we think of 'success'? It is important to identify your WHY, the main driver behind you wanting to be successful in whatever business or line of work you undertake. Some of the most challenging businesses today are in the commission-only selling sector. Unless you know what you are trying to achieve or why you are trying to achieve in those businesses, you will find life is tough. So let's start by understanding what makes human beings tick. Right at the centre of each of us is our identity – how we see ourselves in our various roles. Psychologists call this our self-concept and we all have multiple self-concepts – as a driver, a writer, a parent, a musician, a dancer, a football player, a golfer and so on. If your self-concept is based around the idea that you are good in any or even all of these areas, your performance in each area will be much better than if you think you are poor in each area. Professional sportspeople know this and sports psychologists work hard to develop sportspeople through reliving their successes, visualising how they would like future events to work out and positive affirmations to boost their self-confidence and self-image. It is called 'anchoring' and is a core concept in neurolinguistic programming.

So our first question is, what do you REALLY want your life to be like? How would you describe your 'perfect day'?

Understanding your personal psychology

We now need to think about a few basic ideas about our personal psychology. It is commonly agreed by most psychologists that we have a conscious mind, which gives us our awareness of our environment and an unconscious or subconscious mind which is working away outside our awareness. Psychologists argue about whether this level of mind outside conscious awareness is unconscious or subconscious. Some psychologists even go as far as to talk in terms of the pre-conscious mind. The fact is that no one is either right or wrong on this issue. What is apparent, however, is that we have conscious awareness and then mental processes which are outside our conscious awareness. I choose to call this latter level our unconscious mind. Whilst our conscious mind is relatively limited in terms of its processing ability and memory, our unconscious mind seems to be almost infinite in its ability to store experiences, information and associations, particularly those which are very emotional in nature.

I prefer to divide the unconscious mental processes into two kinds. Firstly, there are the physiological processes such as control of body temperature, sweat response and blood pressure which, unless we have specialist biofeedback training, are not normally under conscious control. Secondly, there is what I call the creative unconscious which comes up with ideas, patterns, interconnections and all the important thinking processes which underpin our creativity. As we will see in a later chapter on problem solving and creativity, we need to engage our unconscious processes to work with us rather than against us. Many people hold negative beliefs in their unconscious which hold them back from giving high levels of performance. We can however deal with many negative beliefs through the power of affirmations and we will return to this topic later. For the present time, just accept that beliefs are not truth but just a set of operating principles which become installed in the human mind for various reasons and in various situations.

It seems that we humans have two types of mental processes: left-brain thought and right-brain thought. Initially these were believed to reside in the left and right side of the brain respectively, but current thinking seems to favour that the processes are distributed throughout the brain (although, at the time of writing this book, the issue is still unclear in many people's minds). The important principle here is that two types of thinking seem to exist: left-brain thinking which is about logic, lists, numbers, structure and numeracy and right-brain thinking which is about patterns, colour, rhythm, interconnections and spatial issues – particularly in the visual sense. In the Western world, our education system seems to favour left-brain skills and those skills seem to be rewarded in the workplace – particularly in the world of business. Accountancy, banking, engineering, technology, science and mathematics all require good left-brain skills

The next issue is to return once again to the idea that you are, in effect, a business with marketing, sales, production, finance, human resource and administrative functions. How effective are you in these areas? If you were creating your 'elevator pitch' to present to some overseas tourists in a fast-moving elevator to the 23rd floor of a business skyscraper, what would you tell them about yourself in 30 seconds or less? Who are you and what are you all about?

Write your 30-second elevator pitch NOW!

My elevator pitch:

When they carry out their strategic planning, businesses have used for many years the idea of the SWOT analysis – strengths, weaknesses, opportunities and threats. We can adapt this idea to use on a personal basis and it is useful for developing self-awareness, particularly if we discuss our thoughts about ourselves with a trusted colleague who knows us well. However, the change we will make is to drop the term 'weakness' and replace it with 'areas for development' making it a SAFDOT analysis. The important point here is that the word 'weakness' is negative. If we dwell too much on what we think we are not good at, we will tend to reinforce those behaviours and get more of what we do not want. Let's be positive and think in terms of 'areas for development' or even 'lesser weaknesses' so that we stay positive and work with the Law of Attraction rather than against it.

What would you say are your personal strengths?

What would you say are your 'areas for development' or 'lesser strengths'?

What do you see as your main opportunities for growth and development as a person?

Can you identify any potential threats or barriers which might stand in the way of achieving what you want to achieve?

How will you deal with those issues?

Exercise

- If you were explaining how human beings tick to someone from another planet, a Martian perhaps, how would you describe yourself using this model?

- How do you see yourself?

- What is your identity?

- What are your positive beliefs about yourself?

- What is important to you?

- How would you rate your capability in terms of your knowledge, skills, attitudes, resources and human network?

- How well do you manage your emotional responses to situations?

- What are your positive behaviours and which behaviours would you like to eliminate?

- How do you impact on the world around you?

- What do you think others think of you?

It is always useful to gain some psychological knowledge about yourself using psychometric questionnaires. However, these can be expensive and so I want to introduce you to just one psychological approach which will give you heightened self-awareness.

This tool is the Myers-Briggs Type Indicator known commonly as the MBTI.

You can explore the MBTI using an internet search and, at the time of writing, it was possible to complete a shortened questionnaire to identify your type. However, if you really want to use this tool, it is better to complete the full questionnaire and then have feedback from a qualified MBTI practitioner.

The principles behind MBTI are very sound and it has decades of normative data to support its credibility in terms of reliability and validity. The basic idea is that we each operate somewhere on four scales:

1. Your source of energy, either talking with others or reflecting alone – the **Extravert-Introvert** scale.

2. The type of data you believe, either specific detail or interrelated patterns – the **Sensory-Intuitive** scale.

3. Whether you focus on logic or on values – the **Thinking-Feeling** scale.

4. The extent to which you are either well organised and structured or a free spirit tending to go with the flow – the
   Judging-Perception scale.

Think about yourself and your preferences. What motivates,
inspires and 'lights your fire?' Is it talking with others or sitting
quietly on your own reflecting? **E** or **I**?

Do you like very specific, structured data with detail or are you
more interested in interconnected ideas, patterns and taking the
overview? **S** or **N**?

When you make decisions, do you do so on the basis of
thinking through the problem with logic or do you decide by
the way you feel about the issue and your values? **T** or **F**?

In terms of the way you live, are you organised and structured,
liking to complete one task before you start the next? Or would
you rather multitask with several projects on the go without
feeling pressure to complete any of them? **J** or **P**?

The Myers-Briggs approach to human preferences enables you
to identify your profile: for example **ESTJ** or **INFP** or any of the
16 possible combinations. By undertaking the full questionnaire
and receiving feedback from a trained coach, it can be very
enlightening. Perhaps its most powerful application is in understanding others, knowing when to talk a lot or when to be quiet
and hand the person a piece of paper. It can resolve conflict
based on preferences. For examples **Js** often think that **Ps** are
lazy and disorganised. **Ps** often think **Js** are control freaks and
obsessive. By becoming aware of the differences in preferences
and acknowledging the attendant strengths of each preference,
we can greatly improve our relationships with others.

Summary

We have discussed the importance of self-awareness, in particular what truly motivates us and inspires us.

What really matters in life is our perception of situations and events and the perceptions we create in others.

There is a clear development structure about how we create our lifestyle. It starts with our conditioning, which tends to lead to the formation of our beliefs which, in turn, determine our response to situations in terms of thoughts, feelings and actions.

This creates our overall attitude, something which all the success gurus agree is an important issue. This has been backed up by research from the Harvard Business School that suggests that the reason people obtain good job positions and are successful in their business career is 85% due to their having a positive, yet empathic attitude.

We can overcome negative beliefs by thinking of what we would rather believe and then associating more benefits and less pain with the new belief.

It is important to realise whether you display a Growth Mindset or a Fixed Mindset and then work towards becoming a Growth Mindset individual.

We have a conscious and unconscious level of thought. We need to engage our unconscious thought processes to work with us rather than against us.

A sound grasp of your 'elevator pitch' will give you focus, motivation, inspiration and a passion for your work.

We can gain a good sense of self-awareness if we think of ourselves as a business and then carry out a SAFDOT analysis.

One way of understanding ourselves and our preferences is the Myers-Briggs Type Indicator which can lead to a classification of personality type. This can help with making our relationships more successful, particularly in a team.

Development questions

- Can you identify a situation where your perception was clearly different from that of another person and you were found to be in error? Why do you think you misperceived the situation?

- What things do you like that you know some other people dislike?

- What things do you dislike that many other people like?

- What is behind the differences of opinion?

- What negative beliefs do you feel have resulted from your early programming and conditioning which affect your performance today?

- What would be the characteristics of your ideal lifestyle?

- What barriers do you feel exist that hold you back from achieving this lifestyle?

- What actions will you take to develop a Growth Mindset and reduce any tendency to the Fixed Mindset?

- What is your 'elevator pitch' and how would you deliver it to an overseas visitor to emphasise your senses of purpose, what you are good at and your passion?

- Can you identify three people who seem to be extravert, three people who are sensory, three people who are logical thinkers and three who are structured and well organised by nature?

• What three steps can you now take to move forwards towards your personal development?

Now please rate your progress for Chapter Two and complete the second mini circle 2 on the dashboard overleaf. Add the scoring for mini circle 1 from Chapter One to update your progress.

Your progress dashboard

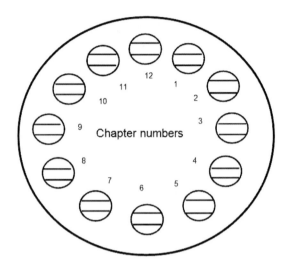

 I understand most of the ideas in this chapter and intend applying those which appeal to me

 I fully understand the ideas in this chapter and having made some progress in applying them

 I am fully committed to applying the ideas in this chapter and have made great progress and I am moving forwards with achieving my goals as I set new ones

Chapter Three
Setting direction

"What you get by achieving your goals is not as important as what you become by achieving your goals." **Henry David Thoreau**

What do you really want?

So far we have looked at the idea that you want to take action to unlock your potential and release the genius that lies within you. There is a way to go about things that will give you the greatest chance of success, whatever your definition of the word; in fact, it will guarantee your success! You have to decide what you want to achieve and then set about putting into action the processes that will bring what you want into reality. Do not worry or get anxious about whether you will achieve what you are aiming for – just focus on getting there. We have already discussed the idea that our world and everything in it is part of an energy field. Whether or not you buy into that idea, it is becoming rapidly clear that our thinking determines our actions and thus our results. Your task is to decide on the 'what' you want to achieve rather than 'how' to achieve it. If you have a strong enough 'what' and 'why', then the way forward will show itself as your selective perception system, the Reticular Activating System (RAS), starts to focus on opportunities which relate to your vision. You will be motivated to take action to explore those opportunities. It has often been said that the human being is a teleological system; that is, we need something to focus upon, a goal, to ensure that our energy is directed and that we do not become sidetracked into unimportant issues. Maxwell Maltz presents a useful background to this idea with his work on Psycho-cybernetics.

What is goal setting?

We are going to look at the whole process of goal setting and how to achieve those goals in a scientific and a creative way. We are going to join the ranks of Einstein, Newton and Leonardo da Vinci in becoming 'whole-brain' thinkers, using the almost unlimited power of the human brain in its creative mode and then structuring those ideas in a way that will cause us to have the right thoughts, feelings and attitudes to carry out the most effective behaviour. In the next chapter, we are going to explore the main ideas that underpin creativity and how we can become more creative. However, for the time being, just rest assured that YOU ARE CREATIVE and that the only thing that stands in your way is your lack of self-belief.

The do's and don'ts of goal setting

What we do know from research on the impact of goal-setting methods is that simply making a list of the things you want to achieve only tends to work well for a minority of people. We have all experienced this phenomenon with New Year's resolutions which, despite being made with the best of intent, fade away around the second week in January. The pattern of attendance at health clubs and gymnasiums supports this situation. Many people make a New Year's resolution to lose weight and get fit by joining a health club but then just do not find the time to make regular visits. There is more to this fact than is immediately apparent. Your unconsciously held self-concept, your enduring view you have of yourself, tries to maintain comfort zones in a variety of areas. Exercise, diet and weight management relate to just one of many comfort zones, each controlled by a thermostat-type control mechanism. For example, if your weight increases you tend to feel uncomfortable, you start watching what you eat and moving around a little more. If your weight decreases below its normal 'thermostat point', then you start to eat more and move less because you feel depressed. What is probably happening is that your unconsciously held self-concept is simply trying to keep you at your normal weight so that you stay in your comfort zone. The best way to manage weight is to decide on your ideal weight consciously then plant it into your subconscious through affirmations and holding a clear picture in your mind of what you want to look like and the weight you would like to maintain. All the people I have talked with who have lost massive amounts of weight in a safe way have done so by changing their self-concept; conditioning themselves to eat more healthily, balanced with moderate exercise.

The unconscious mind is the key to goal achievement

It really does appear that our unconscious mind is the key to helping us create whatever we want to create. There is a process for goal setting and, if the steps are followed, then you will give yourself the greatest chance of success. Many years ago at one of the major American universities, a longitudinal study on goal setting was set up. The graduating class of students all reported the extent to which they created written goals. In fact only around 5% of the graduating students had set written goals. When they were interviewed some 20 years later, a staggering result became apparent. The 5% who had written goals were worth more in financial terms than the other 95% put together. In addition, they had less incidence of divorce, serious physical illnesses and psychological problems. Goal setting is good for people.

The process of goal setting and why SMART goals are just part of the story

So let's look at the process of goal setting and make use of some of the ideas in Chapter Two. Recent management approaches to goal setting have revolved around the idea of SMART goals. By SMART we mean specific, measurable, attainable, realistic and time-bound. However SMART goals seldom inspire people. In fact they may almost appear as a threat, particularly for those with a Fixed Mindset, and that is why there are so many negative beliefs about goal setting which result in the individual not getting around to following the process. These can all become blockers to goal achievement. Positive affirmations are a powerful tool which can provide the fuel to keep the goal-setting engine working effectively and we will see later how to make these work for you.

The useful contribution of SMART goals

Some of the characteristics of SMART goals are useful. Being specific and focusing on what you want rather than what you are trying to avoid is important. That involves the Law of Attraction. Goals require action and take time to achieve. These two issues reflect the Law of Cause and Effect and the Law of Gestation. You need to be able to gain some feedback as to whether you are working towards your goal or in the other direction. Goals should be attainable. Whatever one person can achieve, it is most likely that anyone can achieve if they set about the process in a whole-brain manner. Goals should be realistic and reliable but, at the same time, stretch and develop the person to push new boundaries

Goals do need a timescale or time frame in which they are to be achieved. Lack of a time frame means the goal will not be achieved because we will always be working towards achieving it rather than closure. We need to apply the Law of Gestation.

So how do we build on the good points of SMART goal setting and enhance the process to make it more powerful and hence effective? The key is to add a level of detail and richness in terms of understanding what life will be like when the goal is achieved and then to attach strong emotions to the goal. To do this we will now start to create our goals in the SMEARTIE format. Yes, I know, leadership and management writers seem to love mnemonics but, in the case of SMEARTIE, there is a serious point!

- Goals must be positive and stated in **specific** terms - remember the Law of Attraction

- They must be **measurable** in some way – what gets measured gets done

- They need to be **evidence-based** – how do we know if we have succeeded?

- They need to be **appropriate** and **attainable** – maintaining morale and a sense of progress is important

- They need to be **realistic** and **relevant**

- They need a **timescale** – the Law of Gestation

- The need to be **inspirational** – fuel your passion!

- They need to be loaded with **emotion** to engage the unconscious mind

Now you can see how we can turbo-charge a goal by making it inspirational and loading it with the emotions we will feel when we achieve the goal.

But there is another stage we need to go through if we are to use whole-brain goal setting rather than just the SMEARTIE list of statements: the visualization process to imprint the goal on our right-brain thinking. Emotion gets attached to the pictures we create in our mind and, if we represent our goal with a picture as well as the SMEARTIE list, then it becomes a very powerful process.

The power of the vision board

One of the best ways to trigger whole-brain goal setting is through the vision board. What we mean by a vision board is that we collect pictures and statements relating to what we are trying to achieve and create a collage on a notice board, say two metres by one. My own vision boards incorporate a couple of other ideas which seem to make the process even more robust, making it values-based and giving it some structure. Let's see how that works.

How to create your vision board and link it with goal setting

Firstly, it is important to realise that in today's world we can obtain virtually anything we want. We simply have to decide what we want and what we are prepared to pay or invest to achieve that goal. We need to take into account what is important to us, our values, and the other people in our lives who will be affected by our achievement of the goal. A fundamental statement on my vision board includes the words faith, trust, loyalty, empathy, pride, love and excellence. You can choose whatever words work for you. I then draw a tree whose roots are fed by these foundation values and whose branches represent my goal areas: career, family, finance, leisure, relationships, property, transport and so on. The main branches all lead to my main goal areas and the key words for each goal. Once the structure is in place I then start adding the pictures. You can photograph the vision board with either a digital camera or your smartphone and then print it out to stick above your bathroom mirror, on your car dashboard, on your desk or your i-Pad – wherever it can keep reminding you to stay on track. Any decision you make can then be related to your vision board and you can ask yourself what will help you move towards, rather than away from, your goal.

We are looking at goal setting in both big-picture terms and in detail. The vision board covers the big-picture aspect so now we will look at the more detailed and specific approach to creating a goal strategy to bring the vision into being.

These are some of the basic mechanics of goal setting. Let's set up a system which uses both right-brain and left-brain skills. This process builds on the insight- generation approach presented earlier and ensures that we think through our goals both creatively and logically to create our way forward.

Possibility thinking

1. Decide on your goal areas as follows:

   a) Work and career, family, finance, leisure, relationships, property, health

   b) Now prepare three mind maps which start with: "If anything were possible and there were no limitations, what would I like to…"

      i Be

      ii Do

      iii Have

If you are not familiar with mind maps look up the work of Tony Buzan on the internet. With a mind map you simply write the key word or words of the idea in the centre of a piece of blank paper, preferably landscape, and allow the ideas to flow. Connect up each idea with lines to create a network as they emerge. This triggers right brain processes and helps develop 'whole brain' thinking.

Your mind maps should each have the core statement "If anything were possible and there were no limitations what would I like to ……." and then then build around the things and issues you want to be, to do and to have. Just relax and allow your mind to generate possibilities. Don't judge any of the possibilities as to whether or not they are viable, just collect as many ideas as possible. You should now have three mind maps all with elements from most, if not all, of your goal areas. This will add balance to your goal strategy and prevent you becoming too obsessive about achieving any one goal whatever the cost.

You will probably end up with up to 30 goals which in real life is not workable. So your next task is to reduce the goal topics to no more than seven key goal areas. The best way to do this is to identify those issues which you initially thought would be desirable but now realise you can live without. Do you really want and need that Bell Jet Ranger helicopter and the landing pad on the Sunseeker power boat?! We will return to the fine tuning of your goal list once you have carried out the preliminary reduction exercise.

The Goal Matrix

The next step is to produce the Goal Matrix. We need to create a set of goals which are congruent; that is fit together, complement each other and provide both balance and momentum.

We create a Goal Matrix as follows:

Key word summing up the goal							
	Goal 1	Goal 2	Goal 3	Goal 4	Goal 5	Goal 6	Goal 7
ACTIVITY AREA	1	2	3	4	5	6	7
TIMESCALE							
1 month							
3 months							
6 months							
1 year							
3 years							
5 years							
10 years							
Life							

We then reduce our long list of goals to just seven areas, tangible and intangible, each goal being represented by a key word which we can place across the top of the matrix. We then assign timescales to each goal area and work towards having short-term, medium- term and long-term goals. In this way, we build momentum and balance.

The Power Questions

Then we need to ask the Power Questions. These combine a number of psychological approaches into a practical working set of questions to enable you to examine whether you really want the goal you have proposed. The questions use the pain-pleasure principle, identifying your 'why' behind the goal, the benefits you would gain by achieving the goal, and the problems you would avoid. It works on a sensory level with neuro-linguistic programming questions based on see, hear and feel and looks at the impact on others.

Here are the questions:

- What do I want to achieve?
- How can I create two ways of representing my goal visually,
- (e.g. affirmation cards) to support my goal-related activity?
- How will I show it on my vision board?
- Why do I want to achieve this goal?
- How can I give myself real leverage to achieve the goal?
- What benefits would I gain by achieving the goal?
- What pain would I avoid by achieving the goal?
- When do I want to achieve it?
- Is it realistic and relevant?
- Is it attainable?
- If I had achieved it, what would I see?
- If I had achieved it, what would I hear?

- If I had achieved it, what sensations would I experience externally?

- How would I feel internally?

- How specifically will I go about the task? (tip - work backwards)

- What first action step can I take right now?

- Why have I not achieved this goal yet?

- What roadblocks can I anticipate along the way and how will I deal with them?

- Which of my personal qualities do I need to strengthen in order to reach the goal?

- Do I really want to achieve this goal?

- Who else will it affect?

- What resources will I need?

Once you have examined all these issues you will have truly thought about your goal! You may decide to change it or not to pursue it. The choice is yours. In any case you should revisit your goal matrix regularly and update it at least once a month, or sooner if necessary.

Working with the seven goal areas

You should have a set of seven goal areas which have all been assessed using the Power Questions and are firmly on your Goal Matrix. Now is the time to start assembling your vision board with pictures of items which represent each and every one of the goal areas. Be as creative as you can. Houses, cars, boats and exotic holidays are relatively easy to represent on your vision board. Personal characteristics can be more challenging. Try finding pictures of someone who you think and feel has the characteristic you want to develop. Use affirmations, although not too many as they can lose their impact. Maybe a picture of someone with a perfect body to which you can attach a photo of your face. This is a great slimming tool!

Remember the Law of Gestation. Everything takes time; just as in nature where plants and animals have a gestation period before they come into being.

The final stage of goal setting is behavioural support. Make sure that every day you are carrying out some action to bring your goal into reality and avoid those actions which work against your goal.

For each goal, identify 10 specific behaviours you would have to exhibit on a regular basis to ensure that you are working towards your goal.

Summary

So there we have it. Goal setting is an amazing process which will ensure that we take the necessary action to bring our vision into reality. There is the 'blue-sky' creativity aspect of considering possibilities without limitation to generate a rich set of ideas, then the filtering and focusing process to decide exactly what we want to achieve, and then the process to structure those goals in such a way as they imprint themselves on our subconscious mind. It is about whole-brain thinking: using the creative right brain to generate ideas and the logical left brain to create structure and focus to bring about the desired results.

We have looked at the importance of deciding exactly what you want to achieve and then created an awareness of what it will take to create that achievement. We've looked at the do's and don'ts of goal setting, how to build in inspiration and emotion, and why it is important to remember the power of the unconscious and the Law of Attraction, the Law of Cause and Effect and the Law of Gestation.

The vision board idea has been outlined; a very important way of supporting your goal activity by engaging the unconscious through pictures rather than lists of words. The four-part process of goal setting has been considered: 'blue-sky' thinking, the Goal Matrix, the Power Questions and behavioural support.

Goal setting is a powerful process which results in achievement and makes use of the Laws of the Universe. It is a way of getting the universe to work with you rather than against you.

So, before moving on to the next chapter, please work through the development questions below.

Development questions

- Do you set written goals? If not, why not?

- Have you thought about your goals over the range of areas of work and career, family, finance, leisure, relationships, property and transport?

- Have you undertaken the 'blue-sky' exercise of creating the three mind maps of what you want to be, what you want to do and what you want to have in each of the areas above?

- Do you have any negative beliefs about goal setting which may inhibit your progress?

- If so, what would it be more useful to believe? Then attach more pleasure and less pain to the new belief as compared to the old.

- Have you built in short, medium and long-term aspects to your Goal Matrix?

- Have you identified the behaviours that you need to display on a daily basis to take you towards your goals?

- Have you run each goal through the Power Questions?

- Have you created your vision board? Use an internet search to look up the videos by John Assaraf for some inspiration.

- Do you regularly revisit your goal setting in terms of both the matrix and the vision board to match the changing world in which we live?

Now please rate your progress for Chapter Three and complete the mini circle 3 on the dashboard overleaf. Add the scorings for mini circles 1 and 2 from your previous work to update your progress.

Your progress dashboard

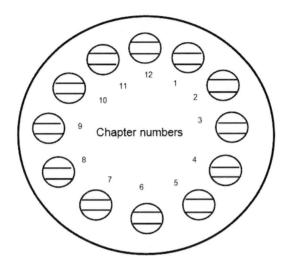

 I understand most of the ideas in this chapter and intend applying those which appeal to me

 I fully understand the ideas in this chapter and having made some progress in applying them

 I am fully committed to applying the ideas in this chapter and have made great progress and I am moving forwards with achieving my goals as I set new ones

Chapter Four
Developing your creative problem solving and decision making

"You cannot solve a problem with the same level of consciousness that created it." **Carl Jung**

We will now continue to explore the energy field concept and start to think about what stands in the way of bringing your goals and visions into reality. Remember it is not just about creating the vision. You have to give that vision 'legs' by embedding it in your subconscious mind and taking appropriate action towards your desired state. However, it is a fact of life that some issues will arise that will appear to block our way forward and solutions often need time to mature and come into being. We all have problems! But are they really problems or just challenges? This is an important point.

Problems are a fact of life

Problems are inevitable in life and invariably develop us as individuals. As has been said many times, what doesn't kill you makes you stronger. So we need to adopt a positive attitude to problems and reframe them into challenges which provide opportunities for moving forwards.

Our language impacts on our thoughts and emotions and subsequently our actions. We need to change our view on what the word 'problem' really means. In reality it is just an issue that stands between where we are now and where we want to go. If we are negative and allow our problems to dominate our thinking so that they become a threat, they will indeed cause us difficulty. However, if we reframe the word 'problem' into 'challenge', or even better 'opportunity', then we will develop a more positive mindset and grow as people. We will start to develop good feelings about our progress and that will impact on our brain's ability to handle our thinking and we will develop a more positive internal biochemistry of the brain and create more ideas.

Worrying about problems

This may seem to be something of a tangent in a chapter on problem solving and decision making but it is not. What is important is that when we try to solve problems and make sensible decisions, it is important that we use our brain as effectively as possible and this involves both creative and logical thinking. If you are in an anxious state, the conductivity of the neural connections in the brain will not be as effective as it should and you will not find it easy to generate ideas. We have already talked about stress hormones and the fact that we need to feel good in order to use our brain to its best ability. We do, therefore, need to address the issues of anxiety, stress and depressed states as they affect very seriously our ability to rise to the occasion of addressing the challenges we face. Depression in particular has tremendous costs both in human terms and to the health system. We need to develop ways to ensure that we stay positive by focusing on what we want to achieve, not on what is worrying us. The more we think about the problem, the greater it appears to become. What we have to do is to focus on solutions.

A real issue with problems is that, in many people, they cause so much anxiety, worry and even depression – usually fuelled by the thought that we cannot handle the situation. This is not just a feature of the modern world. In Lead the Field, Earl Nightingale talks about a psychiatrist who analysed the issue of worry in many of his patients. The figures are very interesting. He found that some 40% of his patients' worries were about things that never happen; 30% were about things that had already happened but about which nothing could be done; 12% were needless worries about health; and 10% were small, inconsequential concerns. That left only 8% being about really significant issues and, of those genuine worries, there were some things that the person could do something about and others which were outside their control. As French philosopher Michel de Montaigne said in the 16th century: "My life has been full of terrible misfortunes, most of which never happened!"

It is important to classify the problems you believe you are experiencing into three areas: problems over which you have no control such as the weather when you have planned an outdoor event; problems over which you have some control such as how you allocate your income in terms of expenditure and savings; and then problems over which you have total control such as the time you get out of bed in the morning. We call this NPT analysis which stands for no control, partial control and total control. Let's get started and create our NPT matrix.

The NPT matrix

No control	Partial control	Total control
Example: The weather on Sunday for our barbecue	**Example:** Reduce the amount of time taken to travel to work	**Example:** Need to lose weight

In the table above, our examples are needing to lose weight as a problem over which you have total control (remember dietary discipline, exercise and choice of foods), the time taken to travel to work as a problem over which you have only partial control (you have a choice of ways to travel and usually where you work) and, thirdly, whether it will rain when we've planned a barbecue. You have no control over the weather! The point here is to tackle those challenges where you have total control first and then work on the partial control problems. This way you will be directing your energy to those things which you can influence rather than feeling frustrated about those things over which you have little or no control – no matter how much you worry about them.

Now draw your own NPT matrix and add your own problems, challenges and opportunities that you feel are impacting on your ability to move forward. Then draw up a list of the most significant issues over which you have total control and then the most important of the issues over which you have only partial control. Then take action. There is nothing more motivating than feeling good that you are moving forwards and tackling things which seem to be getting in the way.

The Multiple Perspectives tool

A tool which helps with complex problems is the 'multiple perspectives' approach where the problem is viewed from the various perspectives of the individuals involved.

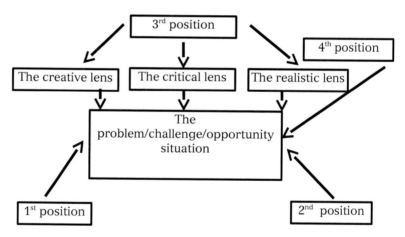

First position is seeing the situation through your own eyes with all the distortion of your personal filters, beliefs, experience and conditioning. Second position is putting yourself in the place of the other people involved in the situation and this key skill of empathy is a very important one to develop. In the training I have carried out with hostage negotiators, I have always worked to involve them in role plays where they act out the role of the hostage taker and then of the hostage victims so that they can appreciate the fears that the hostages in particular have about an intervention or a rescue attempt.

Third position is perhaps the most valuable perspective in terms of gaining wisdom about the situation. We call this the 'view from the balcony' or the 'view from our mental helicopter'. It is the dispassionate view of the observer. As somebody once said, "To observe is power, to judge is weakness." We can enhance our third position skills by using the Disney strategy. Apparently, when Walt Disney was engaged in business planning for his many projects and theme parks, he used to imagine seeing them through the eye of a camera lens. He would imagine looking through the creative lens where anything is possible, the critical lens to identify problems, risk factors and potential financial challenges, and then the realistic lens to consider what is actually achievable. This is a very powerful model and a great way of developing your Growth Mindset.

One final perspective to consider is that of fourth position. This is the viewpoint of a credible person who nevertheless is not actually involved in the present situation. The idea is that you can consider their perceptions based on their experience of such situations unencumbered by political issues or hidden agendas. The Multiple Perspectives tool is a great addition to our armoury of Growth Mindset skills.

Developing your creativity

So let's look at your creativity and see if we can boost your identity and self-concept in this very important area. Once we can develop your perception of your ability to handle problems in a creative way, your belief set will start to move in a more positive direction.

Once we have set your thought processes into motion that you can be successful in tackling your problems, you will move forwards at a great pace.

Below is a list of activities which can help to generate confidence and boost creativity. Consider the list carefully and indicate how often you engage in each of the following:

	Almost never	Infrequently	Moderately	Very often	All of the time
1. Defer judgements of my own ideas	1	2	3	4	5
2. Break away from the obvious, the, commonplace	1	2	3	4	5
3. Relax in dealing with problems	1	2	3	4	5
4. Let one answer lead to another	1	2	3	4	5
5. Generate multiple solutions	1	2	3	4	5
6. Give myself time to consider problems	1	2	3	4	5
7. Trust my own wisdom	1	2	3	4	5
8. Review my strengths and skills	1	2	3	4	5
9. Reject negative self statements, e.g.	1	2	3	4	5

"I can't do it"					
10. Give myself space to create ideas	1	2	3	4	5
11. Take relaxation breaks – go for walks and get fresh air	1	2	3	4	5
12. Try to develop new ideas in a pleasant environment	1	2	3	4	5
13. Get away from interruptions	1	2	3	4	5
14. Use humour to ease tension and generate ideas	1	2	3	4	5
15. Build confidence by seeking out information	1	2	3	4	5
16. Break tasks into manageable parts	1	2	3	4	5
17. Avoid working with negative people while developing ideas	1	2	3	4	5
18. Develop a self-image of being a creative person	1	2	3	4	5
19. Apply strengths, skills and creativity in other areas of life as well as work	1	2	3	4	5
20. Make the challenge fun rather than a threat	1	2	3	4	5
21. Forget practicalities	1	2	3	4	5
22. Let go	1	2	3	4	5

23. See things in new ways	1	2	3	4	5
24. Be playful	1	2	3	4	5
25. Avoid thinking "I'm not creative"	1	2	3	4	5
26. Have the courage of my convictions in the face of opposition	1	2	3	4	5

Reflect on these ways of generating confidence in creativity. Take note of the areas where you have answered almost never/infrequently and think about how you could increase your confidence by trying some of these behaviours.

So what are the characteristics of creative people?

We all behave in creative ways in a range of areas but often take ourselves for granted, so let's now compare your profile with that of people who are considered to be creative. Rate yourself with a mark out of 10 for each of the following characteristics and then total your scores to give an overall mark out of 100.

Involvement with intellectual and artistic activities such as an appreciation of music, art, literature, philosophy, science etc ___

Attraction to complexity and ambiguity ___

Concern with work and achievement, self-motivated, self-disciplined and concerned with achieving excellence ____

Perseverance and determination to reach goals and solve problems ____

Independence of judgement ____

Tolerance of ambiguity ____

Need for autonomy ____

Self-confidence ____

An orientation towards risk-taking ____

The ability to see things from a variety of viewpoints ____

TOTAL

Which of these areas can you develop?

The underlying processes of creativity

So now you have boosted your confidence in your ability to be more creative, let's look at the underlying process. This involves letting go and using both relaxation and even meditation processes. The reason for this is the way we now believe the brain operates as put forward by neuroscience. When an individual is relaxed and not pressured, stressed or threatened in any way, the neural connections in the brain seem to improve in terms of conductivity; in simple terms, our brain works better and comes up with more – and better – ideas. That is an important thing to realise. What we need to do when we want to be creative is to generate as many ideas as possible without judging them too quickly. Premature evaluation prevents conception! If we criticise our ideas too soon, our brain closes down in terms of its generation of ideas, particularly if we give it the message that the ideas must be practical, sensible and workable.

Synvergent thinking

In some ways, this reflects what has come to be called 'synvergent thinking', a mix of divergent thinking to generate possibilities and convergent thinking to focus those ideas into practical action. In graphical terms, synvergent thinking is shown in the following diagram:

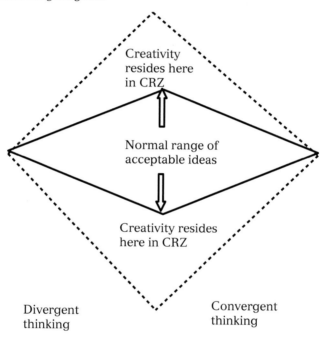

The CRZ, or creativity zone, contains ideas which on their own may appear impractical, illogical, stupid, illegal, immoral or incapable of being used. However, they may trigger other more useful ideas and may combine to create something unusual and, at the same time, useful. Being prepared to ask, "If anything were possible and there were no limitations, how would we approach this issue?" is one of the keys to real creativity.

The lesson here is that we need to open our mind to possibility thinking, whereby we relax and allow ideas to come into our awareness before making any judgements as to their practicality, or how we will implement them. What matters here is identifying the 'what' rather than the 'how'.

So now we have some ideas on how to develop our creativity, let us start to think about applying these ideas to the all-important subject of problem solving – or what we will now call 'challenging opportunities'.

An effective problem-solving process

As well as developing our creative ability, we need to have a logical approach to problem solving – particularly when we are under pressure and our creativity is not as effective as it might be. There are many approaches to logical problem solving but they all tend to reflect some or all of the following steps:

Defining the problem and tuning in to its nature (simple or complex)

Setting objectives on what we are trying to achieve in terms of a solution

Identifying the evidence we would need to show that we had solved the problem

Gathering information and data about the problem

Making appropriate decisions

Applying the planning, preparing and expectation mindset

Taking action

Reviewing the results and making adjustments as necessary

These steps are relatively easy to follow and provide a logical template in which to apply your creative thinking. Decision making deserves a special mention as it is the crucial link between thought and analysis and action.

Some ideas on effective decision making

Here are some useful tools to help with your decision making.

The decision-making process

Collect the facts	- identify the problem - clarify which decisions are yours - decide what information you need - go out and get it
Consultation	- have you missed any facts? - have you got any facts wrong? - ask for and listen to opinions
Think it through	- gather options - decide when you have to decide - be decisive when the moment comes - take the decision
Communicate your decision	- brief people together - sell your decision - confirm in writing
Check the results of the decision	- outcomes - evaluate effects - need for corrective action

The checks and balances approach

In the UK this is credited to Winston Churchill, in the USA to Benjamin Franklin.

The principle is to consider each possible approach to making the decision, then take a piece of paper and divide it down the middle. On the left of the line, write all the reasons for choosing that particular route; on the right of the line, write all the reasons for not choosing that route. Do this for each decision approach.

Write out the possible solutions to the decision quandary:

Solution 1 Reasons for this approach	Reasons against this approach
Solution 2 Reasons for this approach	Reasons against this approach
Solution 3 Reasons for this approach	Reasons against this approach

So what have we learned about creative problem solving and decision making?

Summary

We have looked in this chapter at creative problem solving and decision making. We started by reminding ourselves of the importance of having a vision of what you want to achieve – that is, focusing on solutions not problems. In fact the very word 'problem' can be a problem for some people! It is often more useful to think in terms of challenges and opportunities.

A key issue is the negative impact that problems can have on us in terms of producing insecurity, anxiety and even depression.

The danger with these negative states is that they can shut down our brain's ability to be creative through the action of the stress hormone cortisol.

Most of the things people worry about do not actually happen. It has been estimated that only around 8% of worries are genuine and, of those, there are things we can do something about but others that we are powerless to influence.

We then raised the idea of the TPN matrix classifying our 'problems' into those things over which we have total control, those things over which we have partial control and those things over which we have no control. The aim is to focus on the issues we can influence either totally or partially.

We need to examine the problem from a range of perspectives: our own, the other people involved and the objective observer through the creative, critical and realistic lenses and then seek the advice of an expert not directly involved in the situation.

A logical problem-solving flowchart was then discussed, followed by some ideas to enable us to make more effective decisions.

Development questions

- What do you talk most about, problems or solutions?

- Can you name three problems or challenges you are currently experiencing which you can turn into opportunities?

- How well do you handle anxiety? Can you identify the 40%, 30%, 12%, 10% and 8% challenges with which you are dealing?

- When you create your TPN diagram, where are most of the challenges you face – in the total control, partial control or no-control column?

- Identify two simple problems and two complex problems you have to handle. How will you deal with these issues?

- With the complex problem you have suggested, can you create the Multiple Perspectives diagram in such a way as to indicate the way forward?

- What five actions can you take to develop your creativity?

- After choosing one of the simple problems with which you have to deal, can you create the problem-solving flow chart on page 97 and identify the most appropriate actions to take?

- Can you identify one decision you made with which you are satisfied and analyse it using the decision-making process on pages 98 and 99

- Can you identify one decision you regret and analyse it using the decision-making process as above to see where you could have performed better?

Now please rate your progress for Chapter Four and complete the mini circle 4 on the dashboard overleaf. Add the scorings for the previous mini circles 1 to update your progress.

Your progress dashboard

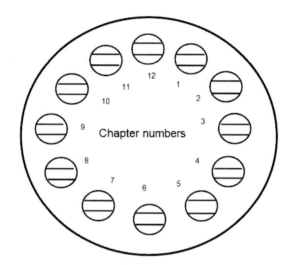

 I understand most of the ideas in this chapter and intend applying those which appeal to me

 I fully understand the ideas in this chapter and having made some progress in applying them

 I am fully committed to applying the ideas in this chapter and have made great progress and I am moving forwards with achieving my goals as I set new ones

Chapter Five
Getting commercial and financially aware

"Annual income twenty pounds, annual expenditure nineteen pounds, nineteen shillings and six pence, result happiness. Annual income twenty pounds, annual expenditure twenty pounds and six pence, result misery." **Charles Dickens quoting Mr Micawber in David Copperfield**

Do we really need to talk about money?

Yes, if you really want peace of mind and to achieve all you want to achieve!

So what is commercial and financial awareness and why is it important if we want to punch above our weight in whatever we undertake? For many people, commercial awareness is about money, being financially viable, and profit. But there is more to the issue than those three basic factors. However, before we look more closely at commercial awareness, we need to clarify our thinking on money and the role it plays in our lives. Whether you choose employment with an organisation or take the high road with your own business, you will tend to end up in difficulty unless you have good financial awareness. This is partly because costs always seem to rise and partly because when we get passionate about what we do we can lose sight of whether or not the situation is financially viable and improving or getting worse.

So what is money all about?

Success with money is not just about accountancy, book-keeping, income and expenditure. It is also about mindset and is a classic example of where the Law of Attraction and the Law of Gestation play an important part in our ability to generate financial success. In many cultures we are embarrassed to talk about money. There is something in our social conditioning that makes many of us reluctant to think or talk about money because, if we do, then we often feel people will see us as greedy, money-grabbing and selfish. This, however, is not helpful for anyone. What we need to do is to inspire people to do things which add value and thus attract money in return for the value they add. If we could do this effectively, then the social benefits schemes in many countries would not be as stretched as they are. Money is necessary to make things happen and we should all be aware of some of the Laws relating to how we acquire money and how to keep and grow that financial resource. Being rich is not just about money, but it is difficult to do what you want to do and add value to yourself, your family and society unless you manage your money effectively both in terms of generating revenue and managing it in the best possible way.

Our conditioning about money

Many of us have been conditioned to avoid the issue of money and to think the subject is a little distasteful. The expression "Money is the root of all evil" is something many of us have heard countless times. However, the true quote is that "The love of money is the root of all evil" and that is a very different statement. The love of money shows itself in two ways: firstly in the desire to amass large amounts of money and secondly to protect whatever money you have against any possible risks.

Deep down we are all concerned about money but frequently lack the big picture and detail skills to deal with it effectively. This is often a feature of entrepreneurs in their early days when they try to do everything, including managing the finances. Their passion tends to push out the financial realities and they are often in denial about the reality of the situation until the inevitable crisis occurs. As Jack Welch, former CEO of General Electric, once said: "Face reality as it is, not... as you wish it to be."

Money and risk management

By avoiding all financial risk we gain nothing and, if we simply stockpile our money under our bed, its value diminishes and depreciates with the passage of time. The same is true of our capabilities and talents in the wider sense. We must use our 'talents' wisely and develop them. Money is not evil but a necessary resource which we need to manage effectively and invest wisely both for our own development and for the good of others. It is a tool and one we can learn to create and use effect-ively.

Let's now think again about the two Laws of the Universe we mentioned earlier, the Law of Attraction and the Law of Gesta-tion. If we accept – as I hope you do – the idea that we become what we think about, then it becomes logical and essential to develop a 'prosperity consciousness' rather than a 'poverty consciousness'. If you keep thinking about debt and the bills you cannot pay, it is often the case that you will tend attract more debt and more bills. If however you focus on wealth and ways you can prosper, you will set up the filters in your brain to notice opportunities to bring prosperity, both consciously and unconsciously.

Similarly it is important to realise that the Law of Gestation means that you will not see instant results of prosperity simply because you start thinking about prosperity. What happens, however, is that you now start taking action to generate prosperity and the processes you set up will take a little time to swing into action.

The Richest Man in Babylon

One of the most interesting books on money is *The Richest Man in Babylon* by George S Clason. You will find more details of this in the Resources section at the end of the book. It contains a series of charming and insightful stories about the realities of money and how it should be acquired and managed, and the mental pictures created promote right-brain thinking. This is interesting as most material on finance is somewhat left-brain orientated and – to many people's minds – boring!"

Clason points to the misery of not having enough money. Without it there is little we can do to develop our position and become what we are capable of becoming. The fact is that many of us today are living in a world where there is enormous opportunity to grow and acquire whatever we mean by 'wealth'. It's not just about money but an holistic concept of being 'rich' in terms of health, happiness, fulfilment and reaching one's potential.

Generating and managing cash flow

The importance of generating an income stream, managing your cash flow and controlling your operating costs is the first issue to be considered. Be careful of whom you trust with regard to financial issues and, once you have started to develop your financial base, treat it as a growing plant. Don't pull it up by the roots on a passing whim! Learn to live on less than you earn, preferably around 70% including paying your taxes. The other 30% can be used for giving, savings and capital invest-ment. Although this seems a tough discipline, it is fundamental to creating a 'war chest' of financial resources both to expand and to cope with the tough times that can arise. Mr Micawber's advice at the head of this chapter is well worth applying!

Think about how you generate your income stream

Robert Kiyosaki in his excellent books *Rich Dad Poor Dad* and *The Business of the 21st Century* has suggested that there are four basic approaches to how we generate our income:

Employee	Business owner
Self-employed	Investor

Employment in a job role

If you just rely on your employment with one employer you are at risk as the world can change and that employment situation can cease to exist. This is happening daily with people being laid off and made redundant in many countries.

Self-employment

When that happens, many individuals start to market their professional services and experience as self-employed consultants and operators. The challenge with this is that we often simply exchange one boss for several and, at the same time, still exchange our time for money. There is a limit to how much time we can give and hence a limit to our potential income.

Being a business owner

Being a business owner is different. Here we earn revenue through the efforts of both ourselves and the people we employ. Whilst this is very attractive to many – "Being your own boss and not working for idiots" – as a friend of mine once said, you are now exposed to significant legal and statutory conditions such as responsibility for your employees, tax, workplace pensions and legal risks if things go wrong. However, a well thought-out business plan can address most of these issues but it does take awareness, balanced decision making and creating good relationships with people to make the system work. In addition, the value that your business adds must be seen to be competitive on the part of your customers and you have to keep up with changes in the marketplace if you are to survive.

The investor

Of the four boxes, this is attractive as it is the closest to the idea of passive income – income you receive but which you do not have to work hard to generate. The challenge however is not to be put off by the idea that you have nothing to invest. Start a small savings and investment programme now. The Law of Gestation will come into play and you will grow that 'war chest' to provide security in the future. One way investors have been successful is through buy-to-let property. Because of the house price issue, many people cannot find the deposit or afford to pay the large mortgages required in today's world. So they rent. And many people choose to rent rather than buy to give them-selves flexibility, particularly in a property market where prices are high but static. Property prices seem to be cyclical and, although there may be short-term price falls, the long-term growth line is upwards. Long term, property is still a sound investment provided the cost of maintaining and servicing the property can be managed. People can receive returns on rental property of up to 12% depending on how they buy, the nature of the property, the local market and a host of other changeable factors. However, most business people agree that, overall, property investment is still sound.

Which box do you operate in?

Most of us are conditioned to be employees. If we lose our job, we look for another job instead of becoming aware of the other three quadrants and developing some activity in each. A phrase which has become very topical, particularly in times of recession, is 'multiple sources of income'. It is about having a number of different income streams which should include some form of employment or state pension, some self-employment activity, creating a number of small businesses, and investing soundly. So give some thought to the following:

- Do you really want to spend all your time working for one employer with the inherent risks that entails?

- What work can you carry out to use your professional skills on a part-time basis? You will need to be careful that your current employer does not have a block on that sort of activity, although this would be unusual unless directly related to your employment.

- What business could you start? Give some thought to a part-time direct selling or network marketing opportunity as these companies often give excellent training, which you can apply to other areas. The financial risks are very small –

many of these opportunities cost less to start up than the cost of putting a sign on your office door! They do all of the product creation and marketing; you just supply the sales legwork and the customers. Although it is not for everyone, it works for many.

- What have you invested in terms of savings, stocks, shares, endowment policies and cash accounts? How are you building your 'war chest'? Start small, tend the small plants and don't pull them up by the roots when you need a cash injection.

Put together, these four strategies will help you to take control of your income generation.

One area that attracts many people – particularly those who live in rural settings but do not want to commute – is the internet. Businesses on the internet range from buying and selling using such services as eBay through to Forex trading and e-book marketing. There are countless opportunities and the great benefit is that with careful planning you can reach thousands of potential customers at low cost. However, as with every business, you should check out any business proposition carefully.

One major growth area, which is becoming increasingly popular with people who want to work for themselves but without the significant risks of funding their own business, is the area of direct selling and network marketing. Although in the past this business sector has not been attractive to many people, things have changed and today's direct selling organisations are ethical and businesslike. They also often provide very high-quality training experiences, which you can use to give you skills to set up your own, more conventional business if that is your aim. To find out more, look up The Direct Selling Association on the internet. It is a very professional organisation representing a significant number of direct selling and network marketing companies where there are real opportunities to generate business success.

So what do we really mean by 'being commercial'?

Being commercial is not about being obsessed with money or trying to stockpile vast amounts at the expense of other people. It is about ensuring that the financial value balance is achieved and that you are receiving an appropriate return for your time and effort and the risks you may be taking. When we talk about being commercial, a number of words come to mind: profit, cash, order book, intellectual property, risk and contracts. In essence you need to sell what you do at a higher price than the costs of producing it, which includes fixed and variable costs and your time. At the same time you need to be competitive and not price yourself out of the market. A very good source of commercial awareness is the book *The Commercial Manager* by Tim Boyce and Cathy Lake. Whilst it will not turn you into an accountant, it will raise your awareness of the financial aspects of your life and your business whether you are an employee or self-employed. The topics covered include the various types of profit – gross, net and operating – all issues you need to understand if you are going to grow your business. Minimising your costs without prejudicing quality or service and optimising your output for the work you are putting into the business are covered.

The key elements of commercial awareness

The first thing is to become aware of the market and how you can impact on the market either as an individual or as a business. Diagnosing what people want and need is very important and then identifying how you can add value by satisfying those wants and needs. What markets do you want to enter? Do you want to be in a particular niche market, a high-price market, a low-risk market or a mass market? Will your financial base enable you to enter the market sector that interests you?

The second issue is the awareness of cash. How will you finance your business? Will you look to borrow from your bank with a loan or an operating overdraft? Maybe you are looking for an investor to whom you can give a portion of the business and its profits in return for their cash.

Think about pricing. The market does not just look at the core product or service but also the expectations of the products and services, what your products and services give compared to the competition and what we might call the 'little piece of magic' about your business and what it can offer. Choose a price which ensures your sustainability and focus on excellent customer relationships by going the extra mile and having your people show a great attitude over the phone and in person.

Take risk management seriously. Identify what are real or objective risks and what are subjective risks, which are more about your thinking than absolute facts. Do all you can to plan and prepare to mitigate risk – and have a back-up plan ready if things go wrong.

The mechanics of financial and commercial operation

It may seem somewhat strange to put this section towards the end of the chapter on financial awareness. I've done this deliberately because the key to effective financial management is to focus simultaneously on both big-picture issues and the detail.

One of the most effective ways I have discovered of developing an understanding of accounts is to undertake a short course, many of which you can find in the business library or on the internet. My own favourite is Finance for Non-Financial Managers by Roger Mason, a Chartered Certified Accountant. He brings the subject to life in a seven-day programme in which you undertake a topic a day. The language he uses and the examples are very easy to understand and, for a relatively modest investment in time and money to buy his book, you can be well ahead of most people in understanding the key issues in financial management.

The key issues in financial management for businesses and individuals

The key issues in financial management are outlined in the chapter headings in Roger Mason's book. Firstly he talks about profit and loss statements. This is about understanding the true cost of what you are undertaking to receive a given return. What emerges for me with this chapter is that in assessing the viability of a business project, it is important to factor the cost of the time you are putting into the project. Profit and loss sheets are important both in terms of businesses and for individuals to become aware of where their hard-earned money is going. A profit and loss statement covers a period of time. On the other hand, a balance sheet is a snapshot in time, a picture of how assets and liabilities relate.

Whilst Roger Mason's book is a great way to gain financial awareness, you will still need a professional accountant who is up to date with tax legislation so that you can claim all the allowances to which you are entitled. It has been my experience that the costs involved in paying an accountant are less that the savings the accountant will obtain for you in terms of tax liability. The book will help your understanding and enable you to hold a meaningful conversation about your accounts when they have been prepared.

What is your working capital and your cash position? What is your position with regard to debtors and creditors? There are many businesses which appear highly profitable but run into trouble because they run out of cash. Individuals can also experience this difficulty by over-borrowing, taking out too large a mortgage and running up credit card bills.

Costing is a key issue. If you are running a business you should be aware of your fixed costs such as office rent, electricity bill, wages and so forth. And then there are your variable costs, the costs incurred with various projects, services and the products you deliver. There are many businesses that produce good turnover but are running at a loss simply because they have not thoroughly analysed and controlled their costs. Remember – turnover is vanity, profit is sanity.

Summary

Mr Micawber's insight on cash flow is fundamentally important if you wish to create happiness as well as wealth! We started this chapter looking at our attitude to money, that it is a resource rather than something to be embarrassed or fearful about. These negative thoughts and feelings about money tend to arise from our conditioning. *The Richest Man in Babylon* provides some charming and highly picturesque stories of the nature of acquiring and managing money based on ancient history. We then looked at the four main ways of generating income – employment, owning a business, self-employment and investing wisely. We should all overcome our tendency just to look at the employment quadrant and explore possibilities in the other three areas.

Remember there is good debt and bad debt. Good debt includes mortgages on your own home and rental properties because that debt is about acquiring an asset which will bring you bene-fits. Bad debt tends to relate to consumables, credit cards, expensive meals out, cars and boats which perhaps you can't really afford. Anything which becomes a depreciating asset and against which you have borrowed can be classed as bad debt because you can never recover the full value. Credit and debit cards in particular, although convenient, are 'plastic' money. They don't feel like real money when you use them to acquire products and services.

Keep positive about any financial problems. There are always ways to find money to sort things out and be prepared to take advice. Remember, as an employee you are always going to be limited in terms of the income you receive – even with bonuses and share options which can sometimes be significant. In the modern world, there are no jobs for life and redundancy is a possibility for almost everyone. Make sure you have a back-up plan that can swing into action if redundancy is a possibility. We all tend to think of our current employment as the centre of the universe. If that job disappears or we are laid off, then it can be devastating. Plan, prepare and expect success in resolving the situation!

Everyone should have a degree of commercial financial awareness and Roger Mason's book *Finance for Non-Financial Managers* is a great way to give yourself a knowledge injection in under a week. We are all managers, even if our management task is to deal with our personal and family issues. If you want to develop significant commercial awareness, then *The Commercial Manager* by Tim Boyce and Cathy Lake is a significant source of excellent material.

Development questions

- Have you even undertaken any sort of training in how to handle money?

- What negative beliefs do you have about money which you have inherited from your parents or other family members?

- What is your attitude to financial risk? Would you consider hiding all your savings under your mattress?

- Have you read *The Richest Man in Babylon*? It is a worthwhile read for the charming stories which will lead you to experience some powerful insights about money.

- From where do you derive most of your income – employee, business owner, self- employed or investor? Divide your income pie into percentage contribution from each of these four sources.

- How would you rate your ability to handle money on the Five Laws of Gold mentioned in *The Richest Man in Babylon*?

- What is your debt position taking into account any money which is owed to you? Can you recover any of that money to minimise your debt position?

- Have you thought of ways to reinforce your self-confidence in being able to handle financial and other problems and become all you can become?

- Have you calculated your net worth, that is the amount of money you are worth based on your assets minus your liabilities?

- Have you taken steps to undertake a short basic accountancy course such as Roger Mason's seven-day programme or one of the many courses available on the internet?

Now please rate your progress for Chapter Five and complete mini circle 5 on the dashboard overleaf. Add and adjust the scorings for the previous mini circles to update your progress.

Your progress dashboard

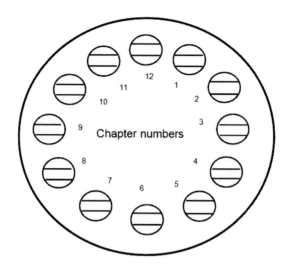

 I understand most of the ideas in this chapter and intend applying those which appeal to me

 I fully understand the ideas in this chapter and having made some progress in applying them

 I am fully committed to applying the ideas in this chapter and have made great progress and I am moving forwards with achieving my goals as I set new ones

Chapter Six
Engaging with others

"I believe in businesses where you engage in creative thinking, and where you form some of your deepest relationships. If it isn't about the production of the human spirit, we are in big trouble." **Anita Roddick**

Human beings tend to be gregarious creatures. Apart from a small minority of people who we call 'loners', we all need to interact with other people whether we like them or not. What we will do in this chapter is to develop your awareness of the various networks of people with whom you interact – particularly those people who you need to help you with your business and life goals. Neuroscience has suggested that we sometimes see others we do not know very well as a possible threat and this can reduce our ability to interact with them effectively. By developing the ability to get on the same 'wavelength' with others through rapport skills, we can reduce this sometimes unconsciously perceived threat and so develop more effective relationships more quickly. If we remember the three main motivational drivers of autonomy and control, sense of mastery and sense of purpose, then this will also help in developing our ability to engage with others and enlist their support in whatever way is appropriate.

Your engagement network

So what is engagement and with whom do you engage? We all have our individual personal networks so simply look down the following list and give yourself a mark out of 10 for how well you think you engage with each network area:

	Mark out of 10
Personal contacts	
Business contacts	
Career contacts	
Educational and development contacts	
Leisure contacts	
Family contacts	
Local council contacts	
Tax authorities	
Accountant and financial adviser	
Legal adviser	
TOTAL SCORE %	

If your score is less than 80% you need to do some work in this area! Select the three areas where you have the lowest scores and focus on developing your positive engagement with those areas as soon as possible. You will reap the benefits! Eventually, instead of you chasing the contacts, they will be contacting you which will make your life a great deal easier.

What engagement is all about

So what is engagement? There are really two aspects we need to think about. Firstly there is the big picture of the networks of individuals and organisations with whom we interact. The second issue is how we handle the actual interaction and whether we create positive outcomes. The business and organisational worlds are placing great emphasis on employee engagement because all the research shows that engaged employees are more likely to perform at high levels, innovate more and have fewer days off sick. In addition they tend to have a better relationship with customers, higher levels of job satisfaction and stay longer with their employer. This is directly relevant to our idea that each one of us is like a business in that we serve others and have others support us just as a business has customers and suppliers of various types. So developing the skills of engagement is a key issue for learning to 'punch above your weight'. Before delving into the skills of engagement however, let us look at an example of one individual's personal network in their workplace:

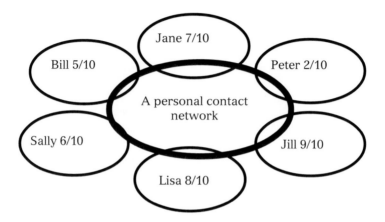

We can see that the individual scores add up to 37 out of a possible 60, that is a percentage of 61%. From this we can see that the person needs to work on their relationships with Peter, Bill, Sally and Jane as they are below the desired 80% mark. It would be unrealistic to think that we can have 100% relationship with everyone but a target of 80% will be very good when we achieve it.

Now think about your workplace colleagues, plot and rate your six most significant relationships.

Interacting with others

Let's now look at the interaction process of dealing with other people. We will look at physical interaction, written interaction, spoken interaction and electronic media interaction.

Physical and face-to-face meetings

At first sight, this would appear to be the most common way we interact and engage with others. However, thanks to the developments in technology, we now have many ways to interact which, in many situations, are easier than actually being in someone's physical presence. In some cases, this has led people to have a preference for emailing others rather than actually meeting them in the flesh. I have been in organisations where colleagues just a few feet apart tend to email each other rather than just going over to see them and talking things through.

Why are we sometimes reluctant to engage with others?

So why are we so reluctant to engage with others and meet face to face? One reason is that it is much easier to say 'no' to someone by email than in person. Another is that we perhaps want to avoid 'difficult conversations', something we will revisit later in this chapter. Apart from the cost and physical inconvenience of travelling to see someone else, perhaps the main reason for increasing avoidance of actually meeting someone can be explained from the research into neuroscience. David Rock, of the Institute of Neuroscience in New York, has carried out a considerable amount of research which I first discovered when I was creating an on-line educational programme on project management. David Rock has suggested five factors which can become unconscious threats during human interaction as a result of the context in which a person is operating. Issues can move from our logical pre-frontal cortex to the limbic system and our ability to think logically, clearly and with appropriate emotion disappears.

The five threat areas are summed up in SCARF – status, certainty, autonomy, relatedness and fairness.

Managing status

A threat to our status occurs whenever someone disagrees with us, puts us down or indicates in some way that they think we are incorrect in what we say or do. This has major implications if we want to develop our Growth Mindset in that being open to feedback is vital if we are going to progress and move forward. One way to handle the status issue and avoid it being a threat to the individual is to ask them questions about their views on the issue at hand. Remember the four stages of insight: awareness, reflection, action and understanding. The context for insights to occur revolves around quietness and security; developing inward-looking thought on the part of the person; an atmosphere which is conducive to producing good feelings; and not working directly on the problem issue. Insights tend to pop up from the unconscious when you are not directly worrying about or addressing the problem and they may not happen until after your conversation has finished.

Managing certainty

Most human beings do not like uncertainty. They like to feel they have at least some degree of control, some autonomy, over their future and when things are uncertain it can become an unconscious threat situation. Neuroscience has given us an insight and understanding into why change and the associated uncertainty is often difficult to deal with. David Rock and Jeffrey Schwartz addressed this in a very interesting way in their article 'The Neuroscience of Leadership', available on the internet and from the Institute of Neuroscience. They suggest that change causes sensations of physical discomfort and that external incentives such as 'carrot and stick' motivation seldom succeed in the long run.

Autonomy, the third factor in SCARF

Modern approaches to motivation have moved on from motivating people through biological needs and extrinsic 'carrot and stick' approaches. For example Dan Pink, in his book *Drive*, proposes that a Type I thinking exists, that is internal intrinsic factors which are much more significant in terms of motivating people than the external rewards and punishment approach. Type I thinking is based on three important motivating factors. Individuals need to feel:

- A sense of autonomy, that they are in charge of their part of the world

- Mastery, that they are good at what they do and developing their ability

- A sense of purpose, that they are engaged in what they do and filled with a passionate sense of direction, mission and purpose

People do like to feel they are in control of their world and, if in our dealings with them we can reinforce this idea, that is great. One of the principles of engaging, enabling management is to make sure that these three issues are dealt with well so that they arouse the emotions of autonomy, mastery and sense of purpose in people who work with you.

It is interesting that when you are in a stressful situation, it becomes much easier to handle if you can find some degree of autonomy and control

Relatedness and getting on well with others

When you meet new people, your brain automatically detects a potential threat on an unconscious level. Once we bond and form a rapport, it puts the new individual into the category of friend rather than foe and the threat level is reduced. In teams which are multicultural, we may have to create the common ground.

Fairness

A fair exchange activates the reward circuitry and this is a key finding from neuroscience. Unfair exchange generates a danger response. Because many people automatically err on the side of the danger response, it is important that we work towards creating perceptions of fairness in all our dealings.

So that is SCARF, a highly practical approach to dealing with people to ensure that we engage with them and their brains as effectively as possible. If you analyse situations you have been in which have not worked particularly in engagement terms, ask yourself: did I in some way threaten this person's status by putting them down? Have I made things seem very uncertain? Have I tried to over-control them? Did we have an unfriendly interaction which triggered the danger response in the other person? Could we have been seen to be unfair in how we handled the person?

On the other hand, if you want to get the best out of people and relax them into the insight state rather than information absorption, say things to reinforce their positive status, provide as much certainty about the future as you can, allow them to feel in control and develop their sense of autonomy, be open, human and friendly and be seen to be transparently fair in all your dealings with other people – even those to whom you do not naturally warm.

The magic of rapport

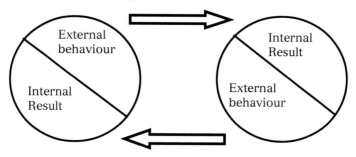

An essential element in engaging successfully with others, both individually and organisations, is to 'get on the same wavelength'. What we mean by this is that we need to emphasise how similar we are in so many respects in terms of thoughts and ideas, what in negotiation we call 'the common ground'.

When we communicate, we carry out external behaviour which creates an internal result on the part of the other person. We may unknowingly be triggering the SCARF factors either in a positive way or a negative way. The importance thing is to become aware of the impact we are having. Our level of emotional intelligence plays an important role in this respect. If we are in a heightened emotional state this transmits to the other person both verbally and non-verbally. By controlling our emotions we reduce the threat level to the other person and we hopefully can trigger their feelings of autonomy, mastery and sense of purpose if we handle the conversation properly. By understanding the emotions of others and handling our interpersonal interactions in a positive, engaging way we will put ourselves into the position of getting the best out of others.

Developing rapport with someone happens through three information channels:

- The words we use

- Our tone of voice

- Our body language

In the middle part of the 20th century, Professor Albert Merhabian of UCLA carried out research which showed that most of the impact we make when communicating with others is through tone of voice and body language. He proposed that the information ratios were 7% words, 38% tone of voice and 55% body language. There have been many misunderstandings about his work, particularly in lecture-type situations, where it would appear that much more of the information is given through the words used. However, it seems that the attitude of the speaker does come across in tone and body language and that is almost certainly the main channel for impacting on the audience.

So what do we learn from this? The key issue is the impact we have on the other person and we need to become aware not only of the words with which they respond through developing effective listening skills but also the tonal and non-verbal aspects. Again, taking the idea of insight creation, if we really want to engage with others rather than pump information into them, perhaps a more useful route is through effective questions to get the other person to think about the issues, take account of the SCARF factors and then do whatever it takes to get the other person to reflect and go through the insight creation process we have already discussed.

Conscious and unconscious aspects

Most of the perception of tone and body language is on a level of which we are not consciously aware. We therefore need to bring into our awareness how well we are engaging with the other person, a process called developing sensory acuity.

So what is rapport all about?

Establishing rapport creates an environment of trust, confidence and participation. If we can gain rapport skills, we can get along with anyone, anywhere, and increase our self-confidence with difficult people. In addition we can make it easier for others to communicate with us.

Here are some points to bear in mind

1. We naturally have rapport with people we like.

2. Establishing rapport with someone enables you to join them in their version of the world.

3. Rapport skills require practice.

4. Notice what people do when they get on well together – they often seem to be imitating each other.

5. Notice when people are not getting on well together – they stand differently, speak at different volumes and speed and so on.

6. When you are not getting on well with someone, try matching their body position, how they are standing or sitting, their words and their breathing.

7. Practise matching to make it easier for others to communicate with you.

8. Liking the other person is not a prerequisite for establishing rapport. What we are interested in is creating effective communication and this is where rapport skills are invaluable.

Mechanisms for creating rapport

1. Use the other person's words and language.

2. Match their tone and tempo of voice.

3. Copy or mirror their body position, posture, orientation, weight distribution, gestures, facial expression, eye contact and anything else you notice. Be careful not to do this in a clumsy way or it'll become obvious! Use crossover matching, mirroring, movement delay and any other device you can think of to become more effective in a natural way.

4. Notice their breathing rate and the extent to which they use eye contact. Synchronise your breathing rate with theirs and match the amount of eye contact they give you.

5. Pace their values.

6. The ultimate test of rapport is when you move and they follow you!

7. Sometimes we do not want to create rapport or we want to get away from someone with whom we have created too much rapport. Simply try to deliberately mismatch the above items and you'll soon see how rapport may be broken. The art of the process is to be aware of what is happening and to choose when you want to establish rapport and when you don't!

Developing rapport with someone as part of developing engagement has to be undertaken with a degree of subtlety. It has to operate on the unconscious competence level, not to appear contrived in any way. I had a colleague who undertook a body language course as part of his training as a General Practitioner. The course was in two parts, firstly the techniques and then the application. His first patient on a Monday morning after part one of the course had a limp and a stutter. He mirrored this patient's behaviour in what was obviously an inelegant, unsubtle way with the result that the patient responded very angrily, accusing the GP of making fun of him. Not a good result! Needless to say, part two of the course put things right.

Shared outcomes

Shared outcomes are one of the key elements of successful influence and engagement. In short, the process is about deciding what you want to achieve rather than what you are trying to avoid. Just try NOT to think of a pink elephant, with a yellow monkey sitting on its back wearing a blue hat! In order NOT to think of something we have to think of it as the brain finds it difficult to cope with negatives. The danger with thinking what we DON'T want is that the brain focuses on what we don't want and then sets about achieving it through the process of the reticular activating system (the RAS). Remember that the Law of Attraction tends to manifest those things about which you are thinking the most.

The ten key questions to engage others

- When can we get together to discuss progress?

- How can I help you right now?

- What can we do to make this just a little bit better?

- What else do you need from me for this project?

- Who can I introduce you to in order to help make this happen?

- Who else can we include?

- What other information can I provide?

- How am I doing based on our agreement for this?

- How can I best support the others in the group?

- What else would be helpful to discuss?

Try them. They work wonders!

The magic of business networking meetings

A really useful way to practise your engagement skills is to attend as many business networking meetings as possible. You can make new contacts, build long-term relationships and learn a great deal from others. Remember to prepare your elevator pitch – your 15-30 second explanation of who you are and what you do – before the meeting and carry plenty of business cards and a small notebook and pen to capture useful information. But do this privately when you get a moment rather than making it obvious what you are doing.

Networking is not selling or badgering but instead it is about increasing your personal contact network. Most of us fear rejection and attending these types of meetings is a great way to overcome that fear. When you attend a business networking meeting have in your mind an objective of what you would like to gain from the meeting and identify specific individuals with whom you would like to make contact. Don't blitz everyone with your business cards as that will ultimately bounce back on you.

Remember to reflect on the outcomes of the networking meeting, who it is that you are going to follow up, and sketch out an informal diagram to show who you talked to. By being a diligent networker you can build your reputation, your business and achieve great things!

Summary

In this chapter we have looked at the subject of engagement as a way of unlocking people's ability to develop good relationships. Employee engagement is a very important subject in organisations and one which brings great benefits. Engaged employees are more productive, have fewer days off sick, are more innovative, are more customer-focused in empathic terms, enjoy their jobs more than disengaged employees and tend to stay longer with their employer. We have extended the idea of engagement to all of our contacts.

We have looked at your personal engagement network as part of the big-picture approach and an example of what your immediate workplace network might be like. The subject of face-to-face meetings has been covered and why, with modern communication technology, we often seem to try to avoid actually meeting with others. One explanation for this can be seen through using the SCARF approach, developed by the neuroscientists and David Rock in particular. We need to be aware of how we are engaging with others based on the issues of status, certainty, autonomy, relatedness and perceived fairness.

We then considered the subject of rapport and how to build it as regards our relationships. The issues of conscious and unconscious communication were covered.

We looked again at the subject of engagement, the benefits it can bring in terms of how we interact and a set of useful questions to ask to engage others.

Finally, we gave some thought to business networking and how to get the best out meeting other people in an informal gathering.

Development questions

- What did you learn from completing your main engagement network exercise on page 122

- What did you learn from completing the workplace engagement network on page 124

- On a scale of one to 10, where one is very poor and 10 is excellent, how would you rate your ability to engage with others in face-to-face meetings?

- Can you identify a one-to-one meeting situation where you used the SCARF factors effectively and created a good result?

- Can you identify a one-to-one meeting situation which was unsuccessful and identify which SCARF factors were violated?

- In terms of influencing others to give their best performance, can you identify a situation where you reinforced the other person's sense of autonomy, mastery and purpose?

- Can you identify an individual who is lacking in one of the above three aspects of motivation? How can you engage with that individual to help them move forwards?

- Can you identify a relationship where you are currently having difficultly and use the principles of rapport creation to enable that relationship to become more productive?

- When have you experienced being really engaged and in rapport with someone despite the fact that you may not have liked them? Have you asked the ten engagement questions to six individuals with whom you work?

- Have you given some thought to planning your next appearance at a business networking meeting?

Now please rate your progress for Chapter Six and complete the mini circle 6 on the dashboard overleaf. Add and adjust the scorings for the previous chapter's circles to update your progress."

Your progress dashboard

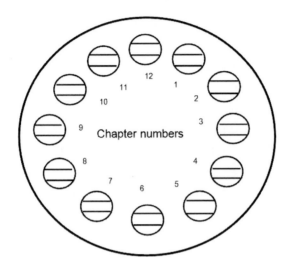

 I understand most of the ideas in this chapter and intend applying those which appeal to me

 I fully understand the ideas in this chapter and having made some progress in applying them

 I am fully committed to applying the ideas in this chapter and have made great progress and I am moving forwards with achieving my goals as I set new ones

Chapter Seven
Influencing and persuasion skills

"The key to successful leadership today is influence, not authority." **Ken Blanchard**

Why effective influence and persuasion techniques are important

Gone are the days of the robber barons who influenced and persuaded others through fear. Granted there are parts of the world where progress still has to be made in this area but, for most of us, the way to achieve our goals is through influence and persuasion rather than coercion.

Going back in time

One of the first individuals to become interested in what enabled people to become influential and persuasive was Aristotle from Ancient Greece. Aristotle stated that to be influential a person needed three attributes:

- **Ethos** – credibility and believability

- **Logos** – a logical argument

- **Pathos** – an understanding of the emotions in the situation

Bringing persuasion up to date

This idea was investigated and brought up to date by Jay Conger who carried out a 12-year research study to look at what enabled managers to be persuasive. He produced a very enlightening article called 'The Necessary Art of Persuasion' in the *Harvard Business Review*, the details of which are in the Resources section at the end of this book.

Jay Conger used three groups of managers and started by understanding how people frequently get it wrong when trying to persuade others. He pointed to the tendency to use the 'hard sell', seeing compromise as surrender, thinking it is just about the logical argument you present and seeing persuasion as a one-shot effort rather than an ongoing process. As a result, he suggested four mechanisms that each of us can use when persuading someone else to a point of view or to do something:

- Establish your credibility with the other person and become believable

- Find the common ground between the two of you in terms of thoughts and feelings

- Present your evidence with effective language and present-ation process

- Connect emotionally with the other person

It is possible to develop each one of these four elements through coaching, training and mentoring and the effort brings about very worthwhile results.

So how good a 'persuader' are you?

Let's see how effective you are at each of the following elements. Give yourself a mark out of 10 where one is very poor and 10 is excellent. Then total your scores to give you a mark out of 140.

Do you plan and prepare when you are trying to persuade someone? _____

Do you think clearly under pressure and when things are uncertain? _____

Do you find it easy to express your thoughts under pressure? _____

Are you a good listener? _____

Are you patient when working at persuading someone? _____

Do you find it easy to win the respect of the person you are trying to persuade? _____

Do you see situations from other people's viewpoints? _____

Do you find it easy to understand other people's emotions? _____

Are you tolerant of other people's viewpoints? _____

Are you prepared to be disliked? _____

Are you good at coping with ambiguity and uncertainty? _____

Do you manage to retain your sense of humour when things get tough? _____

Can you play the role of the 'interested, amused observer' in difficult situations? _____

Do you work out the best possible outcome, the least you will settle for, and a realistic position somewhere in between? _____

TOTAL MARK OUT OF 140

To be a good influencer become a psychologist!

No, I don't mean enrol for a four-year course at your local university! I mean get tuned into some psychological issues. Amongst the many issues and approaches to the human condition that psychologists study are six areas which will help us become better influencers.

Perception

Remember there is no such thing as absolute reality when dealing with human beings. Each of us sees things differently dependent on our biases, personal filters, our conditioning and subsequent belief systems. If you want to be effective at influencing someone, put yourself mentally in their shoes and try to see the world through their eyes – what we called earlier 'second position'. You can develop the effectiveness of your perceptual skills by exercising them and using the Multiple Perspectives tool we discussed earlier.

Cognition

This is about how people think. Is the person you are dealing with a Growth Mindset person or a Fixed Mindset person? How do they come across in terms of the Myers-Briggs scales of where they get their energy – talking or reflecting? What data do they believe, are they logical or emotional in their thought process, and are they structured or 'go with the flow' people?

Motivation

To what extent does this person display the three main ideas of intrinsic Type I motivation – autonomy, mastery and sense of purpose? How can you use the SCARF elements to trigger their pleasure reactions by their seeing the rewards for what you want them to do? Do they respond to carrot or stick? Yes I know this is old fashioned but it is still worth considering, particularly for those people who have been conditioned in the 'carrot and stick' culture. How can you give them variety and a sense of certainty? How can you enable them to feel that they are growing as people and that they are making a valued contribution to something worthwhile?

We need to take into account their personality and temperament

Thousands of years ago, Hippocrates suggested the four types of people. There were the sanguine pleasure seekers, the choleric hotheads, the melancholic detail people and the conflict-avoiding phlegmatics. The words he used don't really mean much in today's world. However, the four aspects of enthusiastic and sociable people, conflict-avoiding team players, detail-orientated loners and bullet-point- orientated leaders still works. There have been a number of proprietary programmes which have used this idea including one called Personality Plus, published in 1983 by Florence Lattauer. If you search for the title on the internet you will find the questionnaire to determine where you fit in terms of the four types. It is a fun exercise to do and the great benefit is that, with a little practice, you can readily identify which box any given individual fits into most strongly and, therefore, how best to influence them. Remember that everyone is a mixture of all four types. It is just that we all tend to display one of these tendencies more than the other three. If you are dealing with the enthusiastic, sociable person make sure you keep things pacey and don't get bogged down with what they will see as boring detail. If you are dealing with a conflict-avoiding team player, make sure they feel safe and free from the risk of conflict. Attend to the small print with those detail-orientated loners and present just bullet points as well as a realistic estimate of risk if you are dealing with the bullet-point-orientated leaders. If this idea appeals to you, it is well worth obtaining Lattauer's book and downloaded the PDF questionnaire from the internet.

Communication

What is going to work best with this person? If they are introverted then they may prefer to read something and reflect quietly on their own. If they are extroverted then a lively discussion may be the best way forwards. Think about what evidence they will need to persuade them. Will it be pictures or words or the feelings they invoke? When you ask them a question, if their eyes turn upwards whilst they think of the answer then they are probably thinking in visual terms and pictures. Use words related to pictures such as 'see, viewpoint, picture' and so forth.

If their eyes go from side to side when they are thinking then they are probably doing so in auditory terms, recalling sounds and words they have heard spoken. Here we talk in terms of words like 'sounds good to me, I hear what you are saying and being in tune'. If their eyes go downwards when you ask them a question then they are either tapping into some emotions or carrying out an internal dialogue with themselves. In this case, slow down your rate of speaking and ask them how they feel about the subject, what grips them about the situation and what questions they might be asking themselves.

Communication is not something you just 'do' to someone. Whatever we do in the way of communication always produces a result and so it is vital that you become aware of the impact of the way you deal with others and adjust what you do to get the optimum effect from the other person or group of people.

Behaviour

As psychology moved from a philosophy to a more scientific footing, the importance of behaviours became significant. Beliefs are not easy to measure but behaviours are easy to observe and this enables data sets to be created so that we can study what promotes certain behaviours and what inhibits certain behaviours. From our viewpoint with this book, the key thing to remember is that people tend to repeat behaviours when they are rewarded in some way, intrinsically or extrinsically, and they reduce the occurrence of behaviours for which they are not rewarded or perhaps punished in some way. Your task in respect of the behaviour of others is to have a clear picture of the behaviour you want to see them display and then do what it takes to encourage them to behave in that way.

Emotional intelligence and influencing skills

As we already mentioned in Chapter Six on engaging others, it is very important to develop your emotional intelligence in the five areas we mentioned:

Emotional self-awareness: We need to understand our own emotions in an influencing situation.

Self-regulation: We need to manage our emotions when working to influence someone else.

Harnessing emotions productively and motivation: We can harness our emotions to motivate ourselves and others.

Empathy and reading emotions in others: We need to put ourselves in the other person's position and see the situation through their eyes.

Handling relationships and social skills: We need to have an effective toolkit of ways to influence others and help them feel good about the situation.

Spend some time reflecting on this range of issues about emotional intelligence and decide on seven areas you will work on improving in terms of your own day-to-day behaviour.

So who was Dale Carnegie?

Dale Carnegie was the person who first put down a significant philosophy for influencing other people. His book is now a little old-fashioned but the ideas, wrapped in a very American approach, still work in today's Microsoft and Apple worlds. His philosophy reflects a number of the issues in the previous para-graph, in particular ego and the need to feel important. Be sensitive to people's needs, particularly self-esteem, and focus on generating an eager 'want to do what you want to them to do' attitude, rather than needing to force or persuade them. Become interested in the other person and create an engaging atmosphere. A pleasant, non-confrontational manner is frequently the way to move forwards in most situations and a smile at the right time can work wonders.

Develop your listening skills and if you are wrong about anything admit it quickly. Don't dig yourself into a hole by defending what you cannot defend. Try to catch people doing something right and comment specifically on that issue. Rather than just say they are a great person, thank them for the effort they have put into a particular activity. Above all, develop your understanding of the other person by finding out more about them and building your skills at being empathic and seeing things through others' eyes.

Unconscious influence mechanisms

Professor Robert Cialdini of Arizona State University believes that we are all subject to influence mechanisms on a daily basis. Cialdini became concerned that, like many people, he was a prime target for fundraisers and salespeople and was often influenced to take actions which he subsequently regretted. He began to research what he called 'unconscious weapons of influence' – ways that professional influencers use to get us to part with money as a result of an automatic 'click whirr' response to the language they use. His book, *Influence: Science and Practice*, has been updated and reprinted many times and is, in my view, one of the most fascinating psychology books even written.

In short, Cialdini believes that there are six core mechanisms that influence us without our consciously realising what is happening. Once you are aware of these, you can guard yourself against them. You may still carry out the behaviour, but at least you can now make a conscious decision rather than just being influenced on an unconscious level.

The unconscious weapons

Reciprocation

The first mechanism, reciprocation, suggests that if someone gives us something it automatically creates an unconscious effect on us that we feel obliged to give something back in return. Commercial organisations do this regularly with free gifts and other inducements aimed at setting up unconscious drivers on the part of their customers to give something back, notably in terms of business.

Consistency

Once an individual has said they are going to do something, they tend to carry out that behaviour to avoid social pressure. This is often exploited by salespeople and fundraisers who will knock on someone's door and say that they are not selling anything; they say they just want your opinion. If a certain article becomes available, would you be interested in buying it? If a scheme were set up to help young jobless, would you be prepared to make a financial contribution? In most cases the individual being approached will say yes without discussion.

The unconscious 'click whirr' mechanisms move into place. When the sales person calls back a few weeks later the individual being approached usually agrees to the request. Unconsciously they have a need to be consistent.

Social proof

This is where we check out whether we should undertake a course of action by seeing if other people are doing the same thing. In marketing terms, the 'click whirr' response of compliance is often triggered by testimonials from other satisfied customers. In less positive situations, if someone is being attacked in the street then many people will pass by and not help until someone else stops to assist. At that stage, several people will stop as that now seems to be the appropriate social response. It is all about finding a leader to follow, someone who sets the scene for what is seen to be appropriate behaviour. When the sales person calls back a few weeks later the individual being approached usually agrees to the request. Unconsciously they have a need to be consistent.

Liking

We are more likely to be influenced by someone we like and to whom we are attracted than someone who we dislike. Hence the use of good-looking people displaying the ideal way of living in advertisements. We unconsciously identify with them in the hope that our life will become like theirs.

Authority

This is related to some well-known research work on compliance by Stanley Milgram, a student of Solomon Asch who taught at the University of Pennsylvania as well as Harvard and MIT.

Milgram's reconstruction of Asch's work is one of the most well-documented and significant contributions to knowledge on the subject of the social psychology of authority. He carried out a street survey to find out if people chosen at random would hurt another human being in the name of a scientific experiment. The overwhelming response was negative. However, when a random group of individuals were placed in a laboratory situation, they inflicted what they believed to be electric shocks on an unknown subject to comply with the white-coated experimenter's instructions. Milgram suggested that the ability to inflict pain on others is within all of us and is heavily influenced by our authority figures, their standards and what they ask of us. This experiment is described in detail in Cialdini's book, *Influence: Science and Practice,* as mentioned earlier.

Scarcity

This is the sixth mechanism that Cialdini identified and it is used every day in marketing applications and the retail world. "Closing down sale – only a few left" brings customers running to avoid missing out on something, even if they did not realise they needed it! We tend to want something when there is a risk of it becoming unavailable.

Influencing decision makers

Most of us have to influence others, particularly our managers if we are in a job, to make decisions. Often we don't achieve the result we want – not because our idea is faulty, but because we do not present it in such a way that it appeals to the mental soft-ware of the person we are trying to influence. A major break-through took place some years ago as a result of some research work by two US consultants, William and Miller. They suggested that there are five types of decision makers:

Charismatics

This decision maker gets very excited about your proposal, so excited that you feel it is 'in the bag' and you don't need to do any paperwork or confirm the decision in writing. You are excited! When you follow up your great meeting, you find the decision maker has gone away for a period and that she or he has not done anything to confirm their decision. You are dumb-founded! You subsequently learn that they had other meetings about the subject you presented with other providers and became just as excited in those meetings. The person who managed to control themself and sign up the charismatic-style decision maker won the business! So what lessons do we learn here?

If you are dealing with a charismatic-style decision maker as evidenced by their level of passion and excitement, stay grounded and make sure you get their commitment in writing. Keep following them up and make sure the relationship is developing. The person using the charismatic style may not be inherently charismatic. It is just the style they use which can sometimes be a deliberate ploy to lull you into a sense of false confidence so that you do not take the action you should in securing their commitment.

To deal with them effectively use words like proven, actions, clear and easy.

Thinkers

This person may seem slow and ponderous. However, in their own mind they are thinking about your proposal. You need to involve them in the thought process that leads to the decision you want them to make. Thinkers often exist in the research and academic worlds and can be quite frustrating as you know what they should do but they don't! Instead they want to talk through options, different ways of solving the problems. Start at the beginning and work through the issues so that the other person thinks and feels that they are part of creating the solution which you are providing.

Use words such as quality, expert, numbers, proof and evidence.

Sceptics

Sceptics can be off-putting at first, until you realise that this style is simply the way they manage to understand ideas and issues. These people are often what we call 'mismatchers' – they compare what you are suggesting with what they already know and feel and they look for the differences. Whatever you suggest, they are attracted to the opposite. Because of this they appear to be disbelieving and disagreeing with all you are suggesting. It is not that you are wrong in what you're saying, but their thought process revolves around differences in perception and so they appear sceptical.

The way to deal with the sceptic is to establish credibility with someone they already trust and try to trigger their positive gut feelings by using words such as grasp, power, suspect and trust. Ground your arguments in the real world.

Followers

These are the reluctant decision makers who are often anxious about making the right decision. As a result they tend to rely on past decisions both by themselves and others to handle the current situation. Use testimonials to enable them to feel secure and present innovative but proven solutions to give them confidence. They tend to warm to the feeling that they have options and multiple solutions.

To influence them use words like expertise, proven results, similar to, previous experience and innovation.

Controllers

These are my favourite decision makers because once they commit, they almost always follow through because they believe the decision is theirs, not one which is pushed on to them by someone else. The secret here is to present the controller with a series of chunks of information which, when added together, show clearly the decision that should be made. Showing the building blocks of the relevant factors and letting the controller put them together to make the decision you want them to make is the secret of influence and persuasion with this type of person.

It is important that this approach to decision-making styles varies between different cultures. The originators, Williams and Miller, felt that American decision makers seemed to fit into just one of the categories. In my own work, particularly in the United Kingdom, I have found most decision makers feature two of the styles predominantly and so I use the two appropriate decision-making strategies together.

If you want to become really proficient at influencing decision makers, then you are strongly recommended to read both the Harvard Business Review article by Williams and Miller, 'Change the Way You Persuade', and their book The Five Paths to Persuasion.

Summary

We have talked in this chapter about why we need to ensure that we maintain our influence and persuasion skills in human interaction to counter the increasing social isolation which technology and electronic communication can create Thousands of years ago, Aristotle pointed to three characteristics of effective influencers: ethos, logos and pathos. Jay Conger made this relevant to the 21st century with his research showing that the four factors that are important in being a persuasive manager are credibility, empathy, effective use of language and understanding the emotional frame in a situation.

We then gave you the opportunity to assess your own effectiveness as a persuader, which will have shown you some areas where you can immediately make some improvements. The six major words that feature in psychology of perception, cognition, motivation, personality, communication and behaviour were then discussed together with their impact on influence and persuasion skills.

We reminded ourselves about the nature of emotional intelligence and the real world of human nature and this led us to think about Dale Carnegie's contribution though his famous book How to Win Friends and Influence People, shown in the Resources section at the end of this book.

Robert Cialdini's work on the unconscious weapons of influence showed us six mechanisms to which we all are often subjected each day: reciprocation, consistency, social proof, liking, authority and scarcity. These are often embedded in promotional messages that impinge on our perception, up to 2000 messages per day.

We then looked at the five types of decision maker: charismatic, thinker, sceptic, follower and controller. Most decision makers are a blend of two of these styles and it is important to use strategies and words that relate to both aspects of their decision-making process.

Development questions

- What percentage of your time do you spend trying to influence and persuade others using emails, phone calls and letters and what percentage of your time do you spend in face-to-face situations?

- Imagine your influence and persuasion ability is represented as a pie chart. What percentage would you assign to your credibility, your ability to create empathy, your effective use of language and presentation techniques, and your ability to understand the emotional frame?

- What steps can you take to improve those elements of the pie chart which are not as effective as they might be?

- What did you learn from your self-assessment as a 'persuader'?

- Thinking about developing your ability to handle the psychological side of life, how would you rate your understanding of the topics of perception, cognition, motivation, personality, communication and behaviour?

- At which of the five areas of emotional intelligence are you strongest and which areas could be improved?

- Can you name three founding principles of Dale Carnegie's approach to interpersonal skills in his book *How to Win Friends and Influence People*?

- Can you name Cialdini's six weapons of unconscious influence?

- Can you name an example of a charismatic-style decision maker, a thinker, a sceptic, a follower and a controller?

- When you dealt with each of the five types of decision maker, what worked and what was not as successful as you had anticipated?

Now please rate your progress for Chapter Seven and complete the mini circle 7 on the dashboard overleaf. You might want to review and update the ratings you gave yourself for the previous chapters when you add them to take into account your successes.

Your progress dashboard

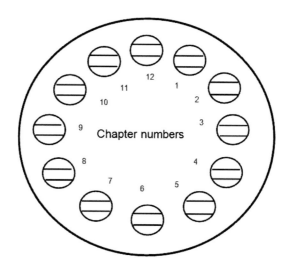

 I understand most of the ideas in this chapter and intend applying those which appeal to me

 I fully understand the ideas in this chapter and having made some progress in applying them

 I am fully committed to applying the ideas in this chapter and have made great progress and I am moving forwards with achieving my goals as I set new ones

Chapter Eight
Skills for selling and negotiating ideas

"Everyone lives by selling something." **Robert Louis Stevenson**

We are all salespeople! You may not be selling second-hand cars, double glazing or bijou residences but you are involved in selling yourself and your ideas to other people. Over the years there have been many excellent writers on the issue of selling skills and we are going to draw upon the ideas of some of those writers such as Zig Ziglar, Jim Rohn, W Clement Stone and Napoleon Hill to help you sell yourself more effectively. For you to be effective at selling, your 'customers' have to know you, like you and trust you and you need to be able to put yourself in your customer's position. Just think – what would it be like to be dealing with you? This issue of empathy and seeing things from other people's viewpoints is key to being good at selling As Zig

Ziglar used to say, "You will get all you want in life, if you help enough other people get what they want."

To be successful in the world in which we now live, you have to have sales skills to get your ideas across to others and achieve your goals.

Our view of selling is created by our conditioning

We have already talked about how our beliefs are shaped by our conditioning and the views of our parents and family whilst we were growing up. These create neural pathways, which give us our interpretation of our experiences including selling. Many people in the past looked down upon the salesperson as someone who was just trying to manipulate money out of them. Whilst this may have been true in the past, in today's world it is simply not true. So let's look at our beliefs of what selling is all about. Remember, you are where you are because of what you've allowed to go into your mind. If you've been conditioned to believe that selling is perhaps somewhat unsavoury, it is time to reassess its significance.

A process for creating success in selling

What matters is that you have a positive belief in yourself to bring about success in selling your ideas, that you are committed to make the effort to succeed and that you will persevere intelligently and not be put off by the relatively minor issues which often seem to get in the way.

If you want the secrets of being successful at any type of selling, take responsibility for the outcomes, be positive, set goals, persevere intelligently and network widely. Be immaculate with your words, don't make assumptions, don't take things personally, do your best and listen. It's not what happens to you in any given situation that determines your future but how you respond. As Jim Rohn said on many occasions, "The same wind blows on us all, the difference is the set of the sail."

Selling is not just about great presentation of you and your ideas or snappy closes but instead is about getting customers to 'know you, like you and trust you'. It's about shifting them from defending themselves from someone who is trying to sell them something and enabling them to move into 'buyer mode'.

APPLYING MULTIPLE PERSPECTIVES TO THE SALES SITUATION

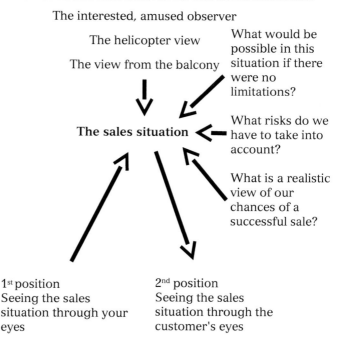

The interested, amused observer

The helicopter view

The view from the balcony

What would be possible in this situation if there were no limitations?

The sales situation

What risks do we have to take into account?

What is a realistic view of our chances of a successful sale?

1st position
Seeing the sales situation through your eyes

2nd position
Seeing the sales situation through the customer's eyes

How to use the material in this chapter

The ideas we are going to talk through in this chapter are valuable whether you are trying to sell professionally, sell your car or house or to sell yourself and your abilities to a potential client or employer.

Emotional intelligence and effective selling skills

We have already looked at the nature of emotional intelligence and the four factors identified by Jay Conger that enable an individual to be persuasive at selling ideas.

Once we have mastered the emotional situation, let's look at how professional salespeople operate. It doesn't matter whether you are selling a car, the services of your business or an idea, there is a process involved. Professional salespeople work hard to have good knowledge of their subject, products and services. They look for opportunities to sell in their warm market of people they already know and their cold market of people they have not yet met. They do not get fazed by rejection seeing a 'no' as one step towards the next 'yes'. In fact fear of rejection is one of the main reasons people lose sales. It is as if their anxiety not to be rejected transmits to the customer and this can cause the customer to become uncomfortable and look elsewhere. One training programme called 'Go for No!' actually encourages people to enjoy hearing 'no' to their proposition. Whilst this may seem counterintuitive, what it does is to remove the anxiety about being rejected and the improved atmosphere tends to bring good results. Access to the 'Go for No' material is shown in the Resources section at the end of this book.

Wants and needs

When selling anything, it is an important idea to find out what the other person wants and what they need. These two areas may not be identical. By taking second position and seeing the situation from their viewpoint, you can start to focus on the benefits to the 'customer' and so show them how you can contribute to the solution of their problems. There are many occasions when people get this far in the sales process but are scared to actually ask for the business. What then happens is that everyone has had a comfortable social situation but no business is transacted and probably none of the customer's problems solved. We will look at closing techniques a little later in this chapter. If a person objects to a specific part of your selling proposition, then that objection can actually hide a buying signal which indicates they are interested but have some queries. It is a good idea to create a list of the main objections you are likely to encounter and then formulate your response to any that may arise. Finally, whatever you sell, do not disappear from the customer's radar! Follow-up is vital to ensure that the relationship will be ongoing and to iron out any minor issues. So let's see how you rate yourself on the sales process.

Do you have a sales process for selling your ideas, products or services?

Give yourself a mark out of 10 for each of the following issues

1. Do you have good knowledge and credibility in terms of the ideas, services or products you are selling? ____

2. How effective are you at prospecting activity for warm and cold markets and refreshing existing contacts? ____

3. How effective and comfortable are you at making the first approach? ____

4. Do you think about the other person and carry out a 'wants and needs' assessment? ____

5. Do you emphasise the benefits and the value you can contribute related to their wants and needs? ____

6. Do you integrate your offer with their wants and needs, emphasising the benefits to the other person? ____

7. Do you ask for the business or result you want to achieve? ____

8. Can you handle objections and be sensitive to 'buying' signals? ____

9. How effective are you at closing and gaining agreement? ____

10. How good are your follow-up skills? ____

TOTAL _____ %

So what are you actually selling?

We tend to get accustomed to our ideas, products and services and the features they possess when compared with the competition and we tend to weave benefits around them. However, customers are not really focused on our ideas, products or services in the same way but, instead, on what they will do for them. They should consciously or unconsciously translate feature benefits into how they and their companies will gain from the product or service. These strategic benefits are called customer gains. Unfortunately, many customers don't have the experience, mental agility or patience to translate feature benefits into customer gains and when you call they are probably thinking about something completely different.

What we should focus on to shift the customer into 'buyer mode' are the key strategic benefits or customer gains that will resonate with the customer.

Closing and gaining commitment

This is a big subject and much has been written on it. Basically it is about asking for the business and there are many closing techniques. One of the best is the assumptive close – 'when you use the product' rather than 'if you decide to use the product'. Be sensitive and not pushy with this approach. Remember we want to trigger 'buying mode' on the part of the customer. Cialdini's principles often work well here – reciprocation (puppy dog close), scarcity (fear of loss), social proof (testimonials – what other customers have found), liking (you should have built rapport and common ground by now!), authority (in your product/service knowledge and experience) and consistency (how your product/service relates to the customer's company's values and reputation). For a really powerful set of ways to gain commitment to your ideas, look at Brian Tracy's 'Closing Skills' programme, available on the internet as shown in the Resources section of this book.

What it takes to be a highly effective salesperson

What knowledge, skills and attitudes do we need to be effective at selling our ideas, products or services to others?

1. Being aware of your current behaviours

   a) Percentage of time listening instead of speaking

   b) Notice the tempo and the volume of the customer's voice and match their delivery style

   c) Don't blame the customer if a call goes wrong – instead reflect on how you might have contributed to the situation

   d) Are you person or product orientated?

2. Build a sound working, mutually respectful business relationship

   a) What is comfortable when talking with friends?

   b) What is uncomfortable when talking with strangers?

   c) Are you creating a 'we' space rather than a 'you' and 'me' space?

3. Create rapport by finding the common ground, common interests and matching the customer's words, tone of voice and non-verbal aspects where possible.

4. Respect the customer's viewpoint and see things through their eyes. Handle objections in a sensitive, effective way rather than building a barrier. Treat everyone as if they are the most important person in the world because self-esteem is a key influencing mechanism.

5. Decide on your outcome for the call and develop a conversation on a human level by listening and reflecting back the customer's words.

6. Practise taking multiple perspectives of your view, the customer's view and then the view from the balcony or mental helicopter.

7. Use questions effectively and listen to the answers. Open questions gain information in the broadest sense, probing

questions gain the detail and specifics, and closed questions are used to gain commitment. Ask yourself questions.

8. Develop your listening skills.

9. Relax and talk in a measured and controlled way by handling your emotions effectively – emotional intelligence is a key influencing skill.

10. Effective time management.

Take some time to reflect on these 10 areas and see what ideas you can come up with to improve your effectiveness at influencing others into the 'buying mode' for your ideas, products or services.

Negotiation – taking the overview

We all negotiate all the time yet few of us ever receive training on being a more effective negotiator. We negotiate at work for pay rises, resources to do our job, with suppliers, customers, colleagues and our manager. Increasingly many individuals are involved in negotiation policy agreements in a wide variety of settings. At home we negotiate with our family members, friends, neighbours, shopkeepers, car dealers and so on. Negotiation is a key part of our lives. In this part of the book, we are going to stand back and consider how to be more effective as a negotiator, obtain the best all-round deals and maintain our relationships so that we can continue to do business in the future.

So what is the essence of negotiation? Why are some people better than others at creating the best deal? How can we be more effective? Insight into these questions comes from a look at the way some cultures treat the negotiation process and we can learn a lot from this approach. Effective negotiators tend to do the following:

- They leave themselves room to negotiate and compromise

- They negotiate with limited authority

- They offer concessions slowly and in small increments

- They ask for something in return whenever they make a concession

- They work towards creating satisfaction on both sides of the deal

- They take their time and are patient

- They tap into the power of emotion during the negotiation process

- They have a clear picture of what they are trying to achieve

The three phases to the negotiation process

These are very straightforward and applicable whether you are negotiating the purchase of a house or working towards freeing hostages from an aircraft hijack.

- Establish the criteria on both sides

- Get information about the other side

- Try to establish the common ground and work towards compromise

Thinking about yourself as a negotiator

- What are you good at?

- What are you not so good at?

- What do you need to stop doing in negotiations?

- What do you need to start doing in negotiations?

- What do you need to do more of?

- What do you need to do less of?

Thoughts from the Harvard Negotiation Project

This has made a major contribution to our knowledge on the subject of negotiation and a number of books such as *Getting to Yes* have become instrumental in helping thousands of people develop their effectiveness at negotiation in all types of situations. Five really useful ideas which I gained from the Project were as follows:

1. DON'T BARGAIN OVER POSITIONS.

We tend naturally to identify our position and then argue for it. This positional bargaining can limit your ability to create a mutually acceptable agreement that benefits both parties. Focus instead on the goal you are trying to achieve and get creative about what you can offer the other side that doesn't cost you much and what they can give you that would not cost them much.

2. SEPARATE THE PEOPLE FROM THE POSITIONS

A great deal of negotiation is emotional and emotion clouds our objectivity. If possible, try to work with the other side as your partner with both of you focusing on a common problem. Don't get too close or else you may start to like them too much and not maintain your own independence of thought.

3. FOCUS ON INTERESTS

Be clear on your interests and those of the other side so that you can work towards satisfying both parties' interests, not arguing for your own position.

4. INVENT OPTIONS FOR MUTUAL GAIN

This is where you need to become creative and focus particularly on how the other party's interests can be met as well as your own. Create a list of options.

5. INSIST ON USING OBJECTIVE CRITERIA

Stay professional and manage the emotions. Agree on standards for how the negotiation will run and adhere to those standards. Use objective criteria and stay cool!

One of the key players in the Harvard Business Negotiation Project has been William Ury who has made a real emphasis on the importance of handling the situation objectively. He suggests a number of key issues we need to bear in mind during negotiation. These are all geared towards changing from uncooperative confrontation to cooperation.

His first point is that "The single biggest barrier is not the other side; it turns out to be us...it's a natural human tendency to react without thinking." He also makes a point about anger, particularly in negotiations, "When you are angry you will make the best speech you will ever regret."

His second point is to step back and take the view from the balcony – listen and be patient. Develop the power not to react.

The third point focuses on the ability to listen and show empathy. Most people think negotiations are about talking. The key skill is to put yourself in the position of the other person. It's about asking problem-solving questions, showing respect and listening – the cheapest concessions you can offer the other side. What are the underlying reasons behind their position?

Number four is the ability to reframe, to see things in a different way. You should say to the other party, "Please help me understand your interests behind your position."

Finally, there is the idea of providing the other party with a 'golden bridge'. Remember that the more pressure you put on someone, the harder they resist. Use a single text or position base, an idea circulated amongst everyone. Find common ground by sharing thoughts and working up a document which shows areas of agreement.

Understanding the importance of your BATNA (Best Alternative to a Negotiated Agreement)

Your BATNA is the course of action that you will take if the current negotiations fail and an agreement cannot be reached. A party should never accept a worse negotiated settlement than its BATNA. Care has to be taken that deals are accurately valued, while taking into account all considerations including relationship aspects, the time value of money and whether the other party will live up to their side of the bargain.

BATNA is seen by many negotiators as a point of leverage rather than a safety net. Most negotiators, however, overestimate their BATNA whilst simultaneously investing too little time in researching their real options. This can lead to poor decision making and unsatisfactory negotiation outcomes.

Things to think about as regards your BATNA:

- Have a BATNA but do not reveal it to the other side

- Do not lie about your BATNA as you do not know how much the other side knows about your position

- Can your opponent really tell when you are lying?

- Should you try to be fair in the negotiation?

- Should you table a 'final offer'?

Concessions

People put more value on concessions they think they have earned rather than those that are just handed to them. Before you make any concessions in any area, make the other side work for those concessions. Value is created in a negotiation when you trade away something that costs you little but is valued highly by the opponent and when you receive something which costs them little but which you value highly.

Large initial demands improve the probability of success. Losers make the largest concessions in a negotiation. Offer as small a concession as possible – be stingy and leave yourself room to negotiate as the process develops. People who offer small concessions during negotiations fail less.

Watch the rate or pattern of the other side's concessions. Do not offer the first concession on a major issue but wait for the other side to do so. A minor concession can be useful from your side as it can trigger the principle of reciprocation. Always ask for something in return. Avoid giving tit for tat or splitting the difference. Choose your own concession rate and keep the amount as small as possible. Avoid giving massive concessions under deadline pressure. Skilled negotiators make smaller concessions as the deadline approaches. A very high, unexpected initial demand tends to lead to success rather than deadlock.

The key attributes for a negotiator are:

- Planning skill

- Ability to think clearly under pressure

- General practical intelligence

- Verbal ability

- Product knowledge

- Personal integrity

- Ability to perceive and exploit power

What are three things you could do to develop your ability in each of these seven key areas?

1.

2.

3.

Key areas for planning an effective negotiation

It is always worth giving some thought to how you will handle a negotiation whatever the magnitude of the situation. Some key issues to consider are:

Background

- With whom are we negotiating?

- What are we negotiating?

- Why are we negotiating?

- Long-term objectives for this business relationship

Stakeholders

- Who are the people interested in this negotiation?
- What do they want from it?

Power

- What is our power base?
- What is the power base of the other side?

Our requirements

- What is our BATNA?

Concession strategy

- What are we prepared to trade?
- What is important to us but not the other side?
- What is important to the other side but not to us?

The other party's requirements

- What is their BATNA?

Meetings plan

- Preparation
- Event timeline

Planning

The most comprehensive planning tool I have encountered for negotiations of all types is the Red Sheet, produced by Positive Purchasing Ltd – a UK company specialising in a range of issues associated with negotiation. The book by Jonathan O'Brien, *Negotiation for Purchasing Professionals*, is a very comprehensive guide to the negotiation process and covers the above issues and the full range of the Red Sheet in some detail. The Resources section has full details.

There are many tools and tactics for negotiations we could discuss, but this is outside the realms of this book. I once contributed to a book of 100 negotiating tactics! However, here are just three that you might find useful:

Nibbling

Here you have agreed the detail and you put your cheque book or credit card on the desk in full view of the other party. "Oh and that price does include ..."(a full tank of gas, a stereo system, or whatever items you have thought of)

The other side says no and so you pick up your cheque book or credit card and put it in your pocket or briefcase. Pause and wait for the reaction. In their mind they have made the sale and they now feel at risk of losing it for a relatively small amount of money.

If that doesn't shift the other party's position, then go to the next tactic.

Walk away

Slowly get up and make your way to the door of the office or showroom. In most cases the other side will try to rescue the situation by making you another offer. They do not want to lose you!

Silence

If you have been creative about the lists of benefits to the other side and all the other steps in building the relationship but end up with a substantial gap, that is the time to use the powerful weapon of shutting up and being silent. The earlier part of the interaction will have involved a considerable amount of communication and the other side may well feel that their position is strong and that they won't give in. Once you have made your offer and they have made theirs, just be quiet. The silence will become unbearable and the first person to break it invariably gives in! As a student many years ago I made a lot of money trading second-hand minis using this technique and it worked every time!

Summary

In this chapter, the point has been made that we are all salespeople, whether or not we warm to that idea. We may not directly sell products or services but we all have to sell ourselves. We are conditioned sometimes to have a negative view of what selling is all about, but we need to dispel that view if we want to 'punch above our weight'. Like most things in life there is a process in selling and, once again, the principles of plan for success, prepare for success and expect success – to coin Zig ZIglar's words – highlight the type of mindset we need to create.

Multiple perspectives provide a useful tool to understand the dynamics of a particular sales situation, whether it is you selling yourself at a job interview or moving on that second-hand car in your driveway.

Emotional intelligence and empathy are key issues in the sales process and you had the opportunity to review how effective you are at the 10-point sales process questionnaire.

Learn to predict objections to what you are trying to sell and decide how you would counter the objection if it occurred in advance. Keep good records of your contacts and call back regularly when it is appropriate. Follow-up the subject of closing techniques – there is a great deal of information on the internet and Brian Tracy's work is particularly useful, see the Resources section for more detail.

You then had the opportunity to reflect on 10 key issues with regards to selling and, hopefully, you have gained some insight into how you can make improvements.

We then turned to the subject of negotiation. We looked at the nature of the process and again we have to remember the impact that our conditioning has on us. In cultural terms we tend not to negotiate for fear we may be rejected. I try to nego-tiate as many prices as possible in order to practise my skill and become used to handling rejection. The printed price often creates the 'power of the written word' which few people will challenge. If you do challenge it, then you can often have a price reduction on what you are buying. We looked at the character-istics of good negotiators and the five styles of negotiation from which you can choose your approach. The Harvard Negotiation Project, and particularly the insights of William Ury, provided us with a useful working approach to any negotiation, including the issues of managing emotions, not overreacting and maintaining our objectivity.

Development questions

- What do you sell? Yourself, your abilities, products, services or anything else?

- Do you have a positive view of the selling process?

- Are you an emotionally intelligent salesperson in whatever context you operate?

- How good were your results on the sales process questionnaire and what subsequent actions will you take?

- How effective are you at making 'cold' contacts and do you prepare the ground electronically with social media or emails?

- How well do you cope with rejection and objections to what you are trying to sell?

- How well do you keep records of your sales efforts?

- Can you identify five closing techniques from Brian Tracy's work or other sources that you feel fit your personality and that you will be able to use?

- What three things do you have to do to develop your ability as a negotiator?

- How effective are you at planning any negotiations in which you are involved?

Now please rate your progress for Chapter Eight and update your scores for the earlier chapters on the dashboard overleaf.

Your progress dashboard

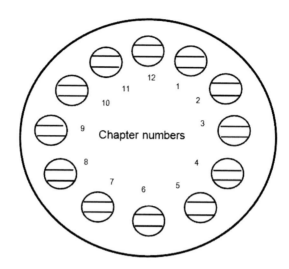

I understand most of the ideas in this chapter and intend applying those which appeal to me

I fully understand the ideas in this chapter and having made some progress in applying them

I am fully committed to applying the ideas in this chapter and have made great progress and I am moving forwards with achieving my goals as I set new ones

Chapter Nine
Becoming a leader

"Leaders establish the vision for the future and set the strategy for getting there." **John P. Kotter**

In order to be really successful at whatever you undertake, you need to develop the skills of leadership. Not just in the sense of leading others but in terms of leading yourself. We have already suggested the idea that thinking of yourself as a business entity with marketing, selling, production, finance, administration, communication and human resource management functions. Imagine what a business organisation would be like if it had no leaders, no vision for the future, no sense of purpose in terms of bringing that vision into reality and no clear set of values about what is important in how you go about your business.

Human beings are just the same. We all need a sense of direction and a sense of purpose and to feel we are good at what we do if we are truly going to reach our potential. So let's see what developing as a leader will mean for you.

Many people think that the study of leadership is a new subject. Nothing could be further from the truth. The ancient Greeks including Socrates, Xenophon and Plato all studied the subject and had their own ideas about how people can develop effective leadership capability. Management on the other hand is a relatively new subject, developing at the start of the 20th century with the arrival of scientific management, work distribution and mass production. What matters in our world today is that we have both leadership and management skills if we are to be successful in our chosen venture.

Our thoughts on leadership shifted in the early 1990s when it became apparent that to operate successfully in an increasingly rapid and complex world of change, the role had become more about developing organisational capability by unlocking the abilities of the people within the organisation than about the old command-and- control style. Admittedly command and control still has a place but is now reserved for just a few critical situations which warrant it. For most of the time, leaders need to be engaging, emotionally intelligent and supportive in terms of getting the best out of their people.

Leader, manager or both?

Many people think that it is in some way better to be seen as a 'leader' rather than a 'manager'. However, this is a flawed argument. If you want to be successful, particularly in business, you need both sets of skills. So let us start off by looking at what leadership means to you and how thought on what it takes to be a leader has developed. Complete the following quiz to see to what extent you are working as a leader and a manager. We can then identify some skills to develop your capability in both aspects of the way you operate.

Choose 'yes' or 'no' to each of the following questions:

	Yes	No
1. Do you spend at least 50% of your time on administration?		
2. Do you spend at least 50% of your time thinking of ways to innovate?		
3. Do you try to 'fit in' to your organisation, particularly in terms of how you dress?		
4. Do you consciously try to be different?		
5. Do you spend most of your time maintaining current processes?		
6. Is most of your time spent on developing people and systems?		
7. Do you focus more on your business processes than people?		
8. Is most of your time spent on coaching and developing people?		
9. Do you rely on a wide range of management controls?		
10. Do you inspire trust?		
11. Do you tend to focus on short-term issues?		
12. Do you focus on a long-term view?		
13. Are most of your questions 'how' and 'when'?		
14. Are most of your questions 'what' and 'why'?		
15. Do you focus on the 'bottom line'?		
16. Do you focus on a range of issues as your success measures?		
17. Do you tend to copy the behaviour of other managers and leaders in your organisation?		
18. Do you tend to set the pace in terms of operational practices?		
19. Do you tend to accept the status quo?		

20. Are you constantly seeking change?		
21. Do you obey instructions from more senior executives without question?		
22. Do you always challenge instructions from above?		
23. Do you strive to 'do things right'?		
24. Do you strive to 'do the right things'?		
25. Do you regularly seek out relevant training opportunities for yourself?		
26. Are you constantly on the lookout for personal development opportunities?		

Total up the number of 'yes' responses to the odd numbered items, i.e. 1,3,5 etc. This gives your 'management' score.

Total up the number of 'yes' responses to the even numbered items, i.e. 2,4,6 etc. This gives your 'leadership' score.

MANAGEMENT SCORE................

LEADERSHIP SCORE....................

My guess is that you may well have a stronger 'manager' score than 'leader' score – unless of course you have already undertaken some leadership development. Let's see how thought on leadership has developed since Socrates' time and through the 20th century to our current situation. For many years people believed that leadership was something possessed by 'great people'. They were naturally born with leadership ability. At the start of the 20th century, the attention turned towards identifying specific leadership qualities which those 'great people' possessed. However, there were difficulties with that approach. First there is little agreement on what are the exact qualities of leadership and how you identify whether or not a person possesses those qualities. So the attention turned towards identifying the qualities required to handle different types of situation. Whilst this seemed initially to be attractive it poses a number of problems – particularly when selecting people to be leaders in a wide range of different situations. Leadership selection tended to involve placing people in test situations to see how they performed as leaders. However, those situations were not representative of the real world and so the process tended to be very subjective, favouring the very confident, outgoing individuals rather than the reflective thinkers. In our modern and increasingly complex world, we need all types of people to be leaders at all levels in our organisations and society, not just at the top levels.

We all have leadership ability

No longer is leadership just for the gifted few! We all have leadership potential and it is the experiences we have in life which tend to determine how far we tap into that potential. So-called 'life events' are very powerful in developing us as leaders; a traumatic situation can often draw on our tremendous personal reserves and we grow as people. If we then couple the insights gained from those experiences with a modest amount of knowledge about the nature of the leadership process, we can all make great headway as leaders. Granted, not everyone is going to end up a Winston Churchill or Nelson Mandela, but we can all move up the scales of leadership impact and effectiveness.

In the 1960s a great deal of research on leadership behaviour took place, particularly in the United States of America, and much of that research resulted in the identification of two types of leader behaviour: actions the leader undertook to ensure the task was completed successfully and actions the leader under-took to interact and support their followers to ensure they were engaged and had a positive experience of the task. This led to the idea of leadership style based on the mix of task and rela-tionship behaviours.

Let's look at the contribution from the UK by John Adair

In the United Kingdom we had a different approach, suggested by Professor John Adair in the 1960s when he was on the staff of the Royal Military Academy Sandhurst. Adair suggested that instead of focusing just on leadership qualities, we should think about what the leader actually does in a situation – that is, what functions he or she performs. This is different from specific task or relationship behaviour and the functions were designed to satisfy three set of needs: the needs of the task, of creating a team and of getting the best out of individuals in the team.

To meet these three sets of needs, John Adair suggested the following eight leadership functions:

- Defining the task
- Planning
- Briefing
- Controlling
- Evaluating
- Motivating
- Organising
- Setting an example

These functions can then be worked through in three distinct but interlinked areas, the purpose being to achieve a particular task and to consider the actions needed to pull the three areas together. This approach is sometimes called the Functional Leadership Approach and, at other times, the Action Centred Leadership approach.

What does this mean to you?

Think about your focus. In leadership situations do you tend to focus on the task but not the team or individual needs? On the other hand are you a 'people person' who focuses on the team and individual needs at the expense of the needs of the task? Do you tend to focus on individuals or the team as a whole when dealing with people issues? An important point about this model is that we have to vary the attention to each circle dependent on the situation and then to ensure that overall, in the longer term, we do satisfy all three sets of needs in a balanced way.

The three levels of leadership

One idea that emerged in the 1980s was the idea of levels of leadership. Whilst there is an infinite number of levels, it is convenient to think of leadership activity in just three:

- **Strategic** – dealing with vision and big-picture issues

- **Operational** – turning strategy and vision into daily activity

- **Front line** – where a group of people deliver specific results

In the past, strategic leadership was the domain of the senior managers, the directors and the people at the top of the organisation. Operational leadership was the work of middle managers, and front-line leadership was about service delivery and quality being produced at the front line to specific timescales with a set of resources.

The world has now changed. With the developments in electronic communications, the people at the top of the organisation no longer have banks of secretaries who will undertake their typing and administration. At all levels in the organisation people send emails, use social media and have to work as team players. Front-line people are increasingly empowered and they can only work effectively in this respect if they are aware of and understand the strategic issues. Thus all three levels are becoming three aspects of one level of personal leadership. No matter at what level we operate in the organisation, we all need to have a big picture – a grand plan – and we all need to do what it takes to put that vision into daily activity. At the same time we all need to develop the ability to deliver specific results and work with others in a collaborative and often a team situation. Thus we will now look at a few strategic issues in preparation for Chapter Eleven, which is about creating your strategy, and Chapter Twelve, which is about creating your grand plan, your visionary big picture of what you want to spend your time doing and what it is you want to achieve.

Relate the strategic leadership issues to your own position

What is your mission, purpose and the direction in which you wish to head?

Have you created the right plan for your development?

Are you putting in the necessary effort to make the Law of Cause and Effect come into play for you?

Are you constantly looking at how you can organise yourself to improve your performance? Chapter Ten deals with this topic in more depth.

Are you fuelling your vision and inspiring yourself by imagining the benefits and wonderful emotions you will feel when you have achieved your goals?

Are you networking effectively with the people who will assist in your development?

As you develop your ability as a leader, are you supporting and helping others who want to do the same?

Emotionally intelligent leadership

We have already looked at the subject of emotional intelligence and the originator of that concept, Daniel Goleman, has researched how emotionally intelligent leadership can be developed at an operational level. He took forward the idea of emotionally intelligent leadership and linked it with the climate in an organisation, which some people might call the 'atmosphere'. We have already covered the issue that neuroscience has given us the evidence that supports the idea that people who feel good about themselves and their work tend to produce good results. Goleman looked at the impact of six styles of leadership in terms of how they impacted the 'atmosphere' in an organisation during normal operations. He found conclusively that in normal day-to-day situations, the most powerful leadership style to create a good, encouraging atmosphere was vision-based, what Goleman called 'authoritative style' where the authority revolves around the vision which, hopefully, is shared by everybody. Other positive styles were the democratic or inclusive style and the cross-functional development style with an emphasis on coaching. What did not work and produced negative results was when the leader was bossing people around, coercing them into taking the appropriate action, and pace-setting, that is proving that she or he could do the work better than the rest of the people. So our learning point here, in terms of normal day-to-day situations, is that effective leadership is based on a compelling vision, getting others involved in decision making, coaching and developing people, and working hard to produce effective collaboration throughout the organisation.

Goleman's article, 'Leadership That Gets Results', is very interesting in terms of which leadership styles tend to produce a positive climate on a day-to-day basis. Which styles do you use? Think about your approach to leadership by completing the following questionnaire.

Reflection exercises

Which of Goleman's six styles of leadership do you tend to use the most and which the least?

Remember for day to day operational situations the positive styles are vision based leadership, including your people in your decisions, promoting effective cross functional relationships and coaching. The less than positive styles for normal situations are coercion and pace setting although they can have a place in challenging or critical situations. Do you tend to coerce people to perform and spend time proving you can do things better than they can?

How good are you at the following in your day-to-day strategic work, daily operations and personal front-line delivery?

Give yourself a mark out of 10 for each of the following issues:

Setting a clear direction by having a vision of the future, a strategy for bringing that vision into reality and a set of values of what is important in terms of how you run the business _____

Have you managed to 'fire up' your team so that everybody is committed to the business in terms of making it successful? _____

Setting an example in terms of how you personally operate on a daily basis in terms of time management, focus on priorities, coping with pressure and dealing effectively with customers _____

Have you created a plan for each person in the business in terms of developing the knowledge, skills, attitudes and competencies they need to possess in order to work effectively both now and in the future? _____

Communicating effectively with both staff and customers. For example, how often do you brief everybody in your team about what is happening? _____

Do you actively pursue a continuous performance improvement programme to identify better ways of doing things and then follow through with the changes? _____

How well do you cope with a crisis? For example, do you try to solve everything yourself or do you try to delegate the problem where possible? _____

How would you rate yourself on self-awareness? _____

How effective are you at delivering results in appropriate times-cales? _____

How well do you handle complexity and uncertainty? _____

TOTAL SCORE OUT OF 100

This is based on and developed from the 'Seven Leadership Competencies' published in *The Business of Leadership by Hooper and Potter* [Ashgate 1997].

Where is leadership now moving as a subject and how can you develop your ability as a sustainable, global leader?

The latest thinking in leadership seems to be around the subjects of sustainable leadership, leading effectively as things change and also the ability to lead in a range of different organ-isational and national cultures. The last point is important as we are increasingly becoming a global village. It is common for people to work for short periods in a wide range of countries and national cultures and we need to ensure that leadership effectiveness is transferable to these different areas of the world.

The essence of sustainable leadership

For a leader to sustain their position, we need to draw upon the thinking on sustainability in general terms. One major research study suggested that global leadership required the ability to handle complexity, understand the context in which you operate, and develop connectedness through all forms of communication media – both conventional and electronic. These form part of the sustainable leadership issues which I have identified in recent years. To be a sustainable, global leader an individual needs to:

- Understand fully the context in which they operate

- Handle complexity effectively

- Be clear on the issues to which they are committed

- Be constantly working on developing people and business systems

- Understand and be able to work in a range of cultures, organisationally and nationally

- Become connected as widely as possible, both conventionally and electronically

So, now you have a broad knowledge of the nature of leadership and some of the key concepts, complete the following sentence by writing about 250 words on the topic of why people should be led by you.

"People should follow me because ...."

Summary

In this chapter we have explored the subject of leadership, which is important whether you are just leading yourself and your 'personal corporation' or a group of other people. Leadership as a subject of interest has been around for thousands of years, yet we still sometimes struggle as leaders in terms of how to get the best out of our people. We looked at some of the issues which are often quoted as differentiating leadership from management and you gained a perception of how you divide your time between the two areas of activity. What is important to realise is that both aspects are important, although the emphasis varies with the situation. We started off thinking that leadership ability was about the personal qualities an individual possessed. Whilst that is still a significant issue, we now think that it is more about what the leader does and how they go about their leadership task.

One of the key issues which has emerged since the 1990s is that we now believe that everyone has leadership potential, although the amount of that potential can vary between people. Gone are the days of leaders just bossing and directing people around through command and control leadership. Leaders now need to operate with a range of styles of which command and control is just one part, reserved for critical situations.

The American thought process on leadership, which developed from the middle of the 20th century, tended to focus on task behaviours and relationship behaviours and the mix of the two areas. The idea is that in normal situations, leaders should operate with a balance of task and relationship behaviour and then increase either task or relationship behaviour for specific situations as needed.

In the UK, a significant contribution to understanding how leaders operate and how they may be developed was created by John Adair with his 'functional leadership' theory of the three sets of needs, often termed Action-Centred Leadership. The three sets of needs relate to the needs of the task, the need to create a team and the need to take into account the individual abilities of members of the team.

We then looked at the idea of the three main levels of leadership operation: strategic, operational and front line. In the past these were often quite different, depending on your level in the organisation. Today, however, we all need to be competent at the processes at all three levels. The people at the top need to be able to create specific outputs, work together in teams and use the electronic media effectively. Those at the lower levels and front line of the organisation need to understand and be aware of the organisation's strategy and feel intrinsically motivated with a sense of autonomy – acting like owners, a sense of mastery – continually developing their capabilities, and a sense of purpose – realising the value and contribution they add to the organisation.

We explored emotionally intelligent leadership and pulled together our thoughts on the core capabilities of leaders which are particularly relevant in the business world.

Finally, we took a look into the future by identifying the six core capabilities for leadership to be sustainable as situations change and we become a global village, working with people from other cultures. Those six capabilities are understanding your context, skill at developing capability on the part of your organisation's systems and people, handling complexity, understanding how to deal with other cultures, getting connected and being clear on your values and those issues to which you are committed.

With all that mental stimulation you were then invited to complete the sentence

"People should follow me because..."

What was the result?

Development questions

- If the results from the leader-manager questionnaire suggested you are more of a manager than a leader, what steps will you take to develop your leadership ability?

- If the results from the same questionnaire showed you are more of a leader than a manager, how will you develop your management knowledge and skills?

- What one event in your life showed you that you personally have leadership ability?

- Do you tend to be a task-oriented leader or a relationship-oriented leader in normal day-to-day situations?

- In terms of John Adair's three sets of needs, do you tend to focus on the task, the team or individual relationships? How can you become more balanced in this respect?

- At which of the three levels of leadership are you most effective – strategic, operational or front line? How can you develop the other two levels in terms of your capability?

- Which of Goleman's six leadership styles do you tend to use most often and which style do you use the least? How will you develop your lesser-used styles?

- At which of these capabilities are you most expert in how you operate as a leader?

- To which of the ten core capabilities will you pay attention in the immediate future?

- Are you a sustainable leader? Which characteristics do you need to develop?

So by now you know the process! Rate your understanding and application of the material in this leadership chapter on the dashboard overleaf with mini circle 9. At the same time give some thought to how you are applying the material of the earlier chapters and update the dashboard.

Your progress dashboard

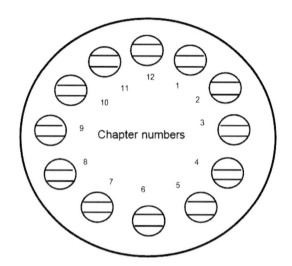

Chapter numbers

 I understand most of the ideas in this chapter and intend applying those which appeal to me

 I fully understand the ideas in this chapter and having made some progress in applying them

 I am fully committed to applying the ideas in this chapter and have made great progress and I am moving forwards with achieving my goals as I set new ones

Chapter Ten
Developing your strategic-thinking skills

"Strategy is a pattern in a stream of decisions." **Henry Mintzberg**

Why developing a personal strategic plan is important

We have already talked about the importance of planning for success, preparing for success and expecting success Strategy is about creating that plan and putting it into action. We also suggested that it can be useful to look at yourself as a business operation in terms of how you handle the key functions of marketing your abilities, selling your ability to add value, developing your production capability, managing finance, administration, and how you manage your human resource – that is, yourself. This chapter takes some useful ideas from the world of organisational planning and will give you the skills to enable you to develop your 'cunning plan', as Baldrick in *Blackadder* would have put it!

What is strategy?

One of the best ways to think about strategy from a personal viewpoint is the idea of POST. We need to establish a clear sense of our **purpose**, set **objectives**, create **strategies** and then the **tactics** to make those strategies work for us in practical terms. It is often suggested that strategy is linked to knowledge and, to a certain extent, that is true. However, if strategy were all about knowledge then those with PhDs would become rich and those without an academic background would remain poor. That is simply not the case. Entrepreneurs do not become rich because of their knowledge, they do so because of their passion, vision, sense of purpose and creativity. Business knowledge and skills can be acquired through the help of others; it is the fire in the 'mental belly' that wins the day. Entrepreneurs tend to become successful when they possess three attributes:

- A mindset of purpose, passion, vision and personal leadership

- The willingness to acquire the business knowledge and the skills they need, either for themselves or through working with others

- Access to a coach or mentor who can act as a sounding board and support system

This book is about all three areas. If you practise the exercises you will develop the right mindset and there is an introduction to key business skills areas which you can follow up from the

Resources section. The book can act as a support system and to some extent a coach, but you should find yourself a role model mentor to assist in your development and maybe coach you through the challenges you will undoubtedly experience.

The basic strategic process

This is easy to understand. It is first about gaining a sound awareness of your present position, your strengths, areas for development, opportunities for you based on your passions and awareness of possible issues that may stand in your way.

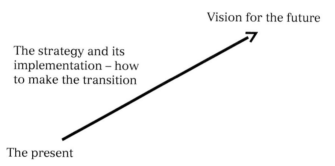

Vision for the future

The strategy and its implementation – how to make the transition

The present

The second key area is defining the vision for the future. We have already looked at this issue in Chapter Three with the concept of the vision board.

The third issue, and the subject of this chapter, is how to move from the present position to achieve the vision for the future – and that is where strategy and its implementation fit into the picture.

How strategy is usually developed

The classical approach to creating a strategic plan tends to follow this process:

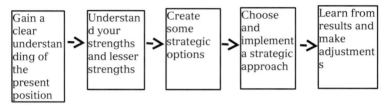

| Gain a clear understanding of the present position | → | Understand your strengths and lesser strengths | → | Create some strategic options | → | Choose and implement a strategic approach | → | Learn from results and make adjustments |

Strategic outcomes tend to exist in one of four groups:

A clear enough end position with no ambiguity about its nature. An example might be to acquire a certain item or exact amount of money, a specific single goal.

There might be a set of alternate outcomes, each different and some dependent on initial decisions. An example might be whether to move house. If you want to stay in the same part of the country, there might be two or more options of where to move. If you choose to go to a different part of the country, there might be only one possible outcome.

There might be a range of outcomes. For example, if you have a travel budget you might spend it all going to one place or combine two or more places in proportions that you choose and based on the same budget.

The most difficult sort of end result is true ambiguity. Let's say you won £10,000,000 on the Lottery and hadn't created a plan of what you would spend your money on. This is a truly ambiguous situation where you have to decide priorities, values, what you really want, who you are going to help and so forth. This type of situation doesn't occur quite as often as the other three, particularly in business, but it can happen – particularly if an organisation is in a dying market or one superseded by technology or resource issues. At that stage, they need a complete rethink with a blank sheet of paper to see what they are going to do for the future.

The diagrams below give a clear insight into these four strategic outcome situations:

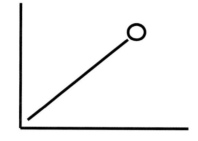

CLEAR ENOUGH FUTURE
Single forecast
Precise strategy
Use traditional tools

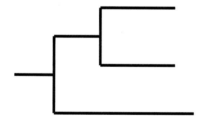

ALTERNATE FUTURES
A few discrete outcomes
Decision analysis
'What if?' scenarios

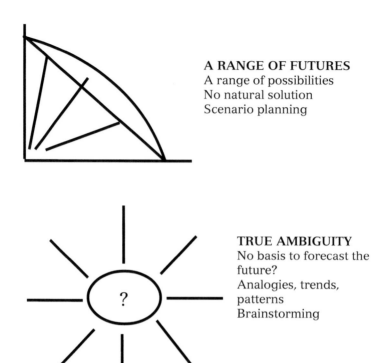

A RANGE OF FUTURES
A range of possibilities
No natural solution
Scenario planning

TRUE AMBIGUITY
No basis to forecast the future?
Analogies, trends, patterns
Brainstorming

The importance of purpose, mission, vision and values

As with any business organisation, the first issue you need to address is that of purpose. What is it you want to achieve? What is important to you about that purpose? How do you think you can set about following your purpose? What do you feel comfortable doing in return for money? Your purpose is basically what you believe is your purpose for existence. You may seek comfort and happiness, create a family, be top of your game in sport, create a large successful organisation or any other thing you truly desire. However, whatever purpose you follow you need to be committed to that purpose, have positive beliefs in yourself and your ability to follow that purpose, and the resilience to overcome the inevitable challenges that will occur along the way.

Your purpose statement (250 words or less)

Why do you exist?

How would you describe your mission? (250 words or less)

In what activity are you engaged?

Summarise your vision for the future (250 words or less)

What are the ten values that are most important to you in terms of how you follow your purpose to achieve your vision:

1.

2.

3.

4.

5.

6.

7.

8.

9.

10.

The elements of your strategic plan

We are going to look at your current position, your intended future vision and the process of getting there. Then we will break down this process into the five stages of understanding the factors in your present environment, understanding your strengths, lesser strengths and preferences, creating some strategic options, deciding what to include in your strategic efforts and then how to monitor and learn from results.

EPISTLE – a tool for understanding where you are now and trends for the future

Work through the following factors and identify the impact they may have on your strategic plan. There are many ways we can consider the environmental factors which are likely to impact on our strategic efforts and EPISTLE is one of the most useful.

Economic – this is about the financial position you find yourself in and the economy around you

Political – the political environment and what government is trying to encourage and support

Information – what information do you need to help with your strategy and where can you find that information?

Social – what are the social trends which provide opportunity for you to achieve your strategic objectives?

Technological – what technological support do you need and what are the trends for the future in technology as it affects your purpose?

Legal – are there legal issues you need to take into consideration?

Environmental – in terms of the physical environment, green issues and so forth, what factors are important both in terms of viability for the future of your strategic efforts and to meet your personal values?

Strengths and lesser strengths

The second area for creating our strategic plan is in identifying your strengths, preferences and lesser strengths. People who are successful are invariably passionate about what they do and are totally committed to their efforts. They do not see work as something negative to carry out to gain the money to live. Instead they love what they do and would do it even if they did not get paid for it, provided they had some other sort of income. In fact some modern motivation theory suggests that if we get pleasure from a certain activity, that pleasure is often reduced if we then start to get paid for it. Human beings can be difficult to understand at times. However, what matters for our purpose is that you identify what it is you excel at and love doing. Do that now:

My strengths, passion and preferences include the following:

My lesser strengths and things to be avoided that don't excite me are:

Creating some strategic options

There are many opinions on what makes an effective strategy. In recent times due to the pace of change, a number of writers have questioned whether it is out of date to have a fixed strategy. Some companies in the hi-tech world even have a saying called 'pivoting'. This is changing direction suddenly because of a new opportunity or even in the marketplace. On balance, the sensible approach to take is that we do need to have a strategic plan to act as our 'compass bearing' but that plan needs to be dynamic and adaptable if significant change occurs.

At one end of the strategy spectrum is the scientific, detailed analytical approach of experts like Michael Porter; at the other end, highly creative thinking as promoted by Gary Hamel. Somewhere in the middle we have the balanced approach of thinkers like Henry Mintzberg. His Emergent Strategy model is a realistic one which makes an important point.

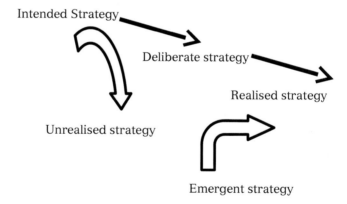

Intended Strategy

Deliberate strategy

Realised strategy

Unrealised strategy

Emergent strategy

Mintzberg's model is interesting because it suggests that we start off with an intended strategy which we then formalise into a deliberate strategy. Along the way certain things can often fail to happen which is called unrealised strategy. Our strategic course can change because new issues arise which become what we call emergent strategy and what we ultimately achieve is realised strategy.

So, what is your intended strategy?

Can you anticipate any parts of that strategy that might not come about – your unrealised strategy?

Taking those into account, what do you think your deliberate strategy will look like?

What emergent strategy might develop along the way?

What do you think will be your realised strategy?

Whilst you may find it difficult to be specific about your answers, the fact that you are thinking about these issues will enable your thinking to be more strategic.

Choosing and implementing a strategic approach

This is where you have to make real decisions about the way ahead. Some strategic options will be more attractive than others. The decision-making tools of Chapter Four can be useful in this respect. However, there is one tool suggested by Bill Grundy in his book *Gurus on Business Strategy* which is as useful for individuals as it is for business organisations. I call this the option-criteria approach.

The idea is to list your strategic options across the top of the page (in the figure, four options have been identified) and then decide on various criteria you will use to evaluate the attractiveness of that option. Examples of these criteria are given below.

Option Criteria	Option 1	Option 2	Option 3	Option 4
Strategic attractiveness				
Acceptability to stakeholders				
Financial attractiveness				
Difficulty of implementation				
Uncertainty and risk				
TOTAL SCORE				

You can score each option out of 10 points where 10 is totally positive and then total the score for each column. This is very much a left-brain approach and you may find that although you obtain an answer which is logical, it may not appeal to your intuition. At this point you need to take time out to reflect on the range of options and the criteria you have identified. Maybe there are some criteria issues you have not yet included. More likely is the fact that on an unconscious level you may have doubts or even a competing commitment that could hold you back. Take time to reflect and try to gain some insight on the strategic options issue. Your unconscious will eventually come to your assistance with a solution that will match both your logical analysis and your intuitive sense. This process is helped by suggesting to yourself that by a certain time the answer will come to you. It is the same principle we use when we have to get up unusually early, say to catch a flight, and set two or three alarm clocks to ensure we wake up. I usually find I wake up a minute or so before the first alarm clock sounds! Your unconscious can be very powerful in this respect with decision making. Your conscious mind is only a fraction of your mental capability, your unconscious is massive in comparison. You will make better decisions if you learn to engage with your unconscious rather than allow it to harbour hidden objections to your progress in order to keep you in your comfort zone.

Learning from your results and making adjustments

It is seldom the case that we get things 100% right first time. All systems which are successful note their outputs and compare them with what they set out to achieve. They then work on the differences to bring the actual output closer to the desired output. If we as humans want to be the same, we have to do likewise. What we do know from modern psychological thought is that there are successful ways of dealing with positive and negative results and unsuccessful ways of dealing with both types of situation. Dealing with feedback is important, particularly if you want to develop a Growth Mindset. These are the options:

The positive way to deal with success	The positive way to deal with less than success
Treat it as permanent and enduring	Treat it as specific to just this situation
It's the action that you and your people took	It is due to a mix of internal action and external circumstances
It can be related to everything we do	It is just temporary to this particular situation

These are the sorts of messages you hear from people who do not handle feedback well:

The negative way to deal with success	The negative way to deal with less than success
It is just specific to this situation	We always seem to fail at everything
It was due to external factors	It was our fault entirely
It will be short-lived	Everything seems to go wrong

So when things do not go as planned, do not just switch into blame frame and try to find someone on whom you can place the responsibility for the problem. Focus instead on the outcome you would rather have. The Laws of the Universe are just as important in strategic thinking as in normal day-to-day activity. The Law of Attraction tells us to focus on what we want, not what we want to avoid. The Law of Gestation reminds us that things take time to swing into action, often with learning along the way. The Law of Cause and Effect means we have to take action to achieve the results we seek. Many people make the mistake of thinking you just have to create your strategic vision and everything will happen almost by magic. The vision opens up your selective perception to identify opportunities related to your vision and then you have to act on those opportunities and follow through until you have realised your vision.

How the changes in thinking on business strategy can help you

We have already raised the idea that some business experts think that conventional strategy is somewhat outdated to the rapid rate of change we seem to be experiencing. Not everyone thinks like that. One of the most interesting developments in strategic thinking for organisations is Blue Ocean Strategy which has emerged from the Harvard Business School and is featured in a book of that name written by W. Chan Kim and Renee Mauborgne, who are both professors of strategy and management at INSEAD in France. They make a number of useful points that are just as relevant for individuals wanting to be successful as they are for businesses.

Firstly, don't compete with your rivals, make them irrelevant. Avoid competition by doing something different in what they term the Blue Ocean rather than the Red Ocean of competitiveness. They give some great examples of organisations who have done this. For example, Cirque du Soleil has repositioned the circus to be a theatrical event rather than one which offended animal rights groups. As a result, the company has expanded and created massive revenues which conventional circus organisations were finding it increasingly hard to do. It is about creating ongoing innovation and what is called value innovation. This places equal emphasis on value and innovation as its name implies and the result is the attraction of a whole new range of customers as Cirque du Soleil has discovered.

Blue Ocean strategy is also about reconstructing market boundaries, focusing on the big picture not just profit or the numbers, it is about reaching beyond existing demand and getting the strategic sequence right. If you are keen to develop your own business, it is strongly recommended that you obtain a copy of *Blue Ocean Strategy* and devour it!

A final thought

Remember that although strategic, big-picture thinking is vitally important for creating and sustaining success, you also have to focus on what you actually deliver and ensure that you get the details right. In helping you to achieve that, the next chapter will look at the issue of high-performance working without the often associated problems of pressure and stress. In the meantime, let us review what we have covered in this chapter.

Summary

In this chapter, we have emphasised the importance of being strategic in your thinking and in planning for success, preparing for success and expecting success. It is about vision, mindset, expectation, belief and action. We have again compared ourselves to a business organisation to give us some key ideas on areas we need to develop and we need to do this in a balanced way.

We talked in terms of strategy as the POST idea of purpose, objectives, strategies and tactics. In this chapter we have focused on the first three issues and we will deal with the tactical issue in the next chapter. We noted that entrepreneurs tend to become successful when they have: purpose, passion, vision and innovation; access to business knowledge and skills; supporting activity of coaching and mentoring; and contact with effective role models who have themselves achieved success.

We looked at the basic strategic process of understanding your present position, creating your vision for the future and then the transition to get from where you are now to where you want to get. We then expanded this into five stages with some thoughts on how you could develop each stage. In particular we looked at the nature of four different types of future vision.

As with a business, the successful individual profits by having a clear purpose, sense of mission, a vision and a set of values to which they work. Time spent clarifying these things in your own mind is never wasted and you are encouraged to answer the questions on page 205 and 206.

EPISTLE provides a useful way of looking at your present context and we then moved on to thinking about what you want to spend your time doing in terms of your strengths, passion and preferences. We need to acknowledge what are our lesser strengths but the Law of Attraction reminds us that we must not think too much about these or else we could encourage them to develop.

We looked at the different types of strategy in Henry Mintzberg's Emergent Strategy model: intended, unrealised, emergent, deliberate and realised.

The option-criteria grid will help you choose the right strategy. This compares the advantages and disadvantages of a range of strategic options. We were reminded that this approach is very 'left brain' and we need somehow to involve our unconscious thought processes, which is where a great deal of the human brain's mental capability lies.

We then looked at the process of learning from the outputs you have created and dealing with both successes and outcomes which are not successful.

Finally, you were pointed in the direction of Blue Ocean Strategy which is about innovation and creating new ground rather than competing with existing people and organisations.

Development questions

- On a scale of one to 10, where 10 is excellent, how would you rate your ability to be objective and strategic in your thinking?

- Have you identified at least three positive role models with whom you can talk through your career or business development?

- Which of the four strategic outcomes on page 203 and 204 matches the situation with which you have to deal at the present time?

- Have you written out your purpose, mission, vision and value statements and placed them in a position where you can read them every day?

- What did your EPISTLE analysis reveal that you had not been aware of before you undertook it?

- Do you have a clear view of your strengths and core competencies?

- Please complete the option-criteria matrix shown on page 211 for your career or business. To what strategic direction does it lead you?

- How well do you deal with feedback? Give three examples of where you have handled success well and where you have handled less than success well.

- Can you identify a job or business area that is Blue Ocean in nature and in which you would like to get involved? What action will you take to achieve this aim?

- How will you continue to feed your passion, sense of mission and purpose and live a balanced life?

Now please rate your progress for Chapter Ten on the dash-board by completing mini circle 10. Review your ratings for the past chapters.

Your progress dashboard

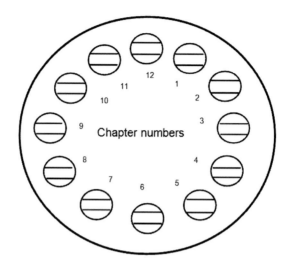

Chapter numbers

 I understand most of the ideas in this chapter and intend applying those which appeal to me

 I fully understand the ideas in this chapter and having made some progress in applying them

 I am fully committed to applying the ideas in this chapter and have made great progress and I am moving forwards with achieving my goals as I set new ones

Chapter Eleven
Becoming a peak performer

"The secret of getting ahead is getting started. The secret of getting started is breaking your complex overwhelming tasks into small manageable tasks, and then starting on the first one." **Mark Twain**

So what is a peak performer?

Peak performance is a subject which has interested us for many years and there are many case studies which have tried to identify the specific characteristics of a peak performer. An interesting contribution to our knowledge on this subject was made by Charles Garfield in his book Peak Performers, as shown in the Resources section at the end of this book, which is well worth reading for any serious student of personal performance development. Garfield is a behavioural scientist and psychologist who worked on the Apollo 11 project where he had the opportunity to study peak performers. One particularly useful result of his work was the identification of six areas which characterise peak performers – whether they are astronauts, engineers, musicians, business executives or people employed in the public and third sectors. He proposed that peak performers:

- Have a compelling sense of purpose, a mission that motivates

- They create outstanding results in real time

- They operate effective self-management through self-mastery

- They work well in collaboration with others and have team player skills and gain leverage through working with others effectively

- They have the ability to make course corrections as a result of feedback

- They are masters at managing change through anticipating change, adapting and taking appropriate action

If you take stock for a moment, you will see that we have already addressed these issues through identifying your purpose, developing your goal setting and achieving skills, developing your skills to gain self-mastery in a number of areas, skills for engaging with others, handling feedback and dealing with change. We can further sum up all these ideas with the notion of intrinsic motivation based on purpose, mastery and autonomy – taking charge of your life and the direction in which you are heading. In this chapter, we are going to develop these skills further and enable you to create a way of working that will bring many benefits, tangible and intangible.

So how do you rate as a peak performer on these six stages?

Give yourself a mark out of 10 where 10 is great and one is very poor.

I have a compelling sense of purpose that drives me _____

I create excellent results in short timescales _____

I am excellent at all the areas of competence I need to meet my purpose _____

I work well with others and they give me leverage to my efforts _____

I thrive on feedback and am pleased to make necessary course corrections _____

Change excites me as I anticipate, adapt and then take the necessary actions _____

TOTAL MARK OUT OF 60

Garfield suggests that to develop your ability as a peak performer you need to work on four issues:

- Keep learning new things and ways of working

- Build your positive expectation of success

- Map out your desired future

- Update your mission and purpose as the world about you moves on

Understanding human performance

An interesting idea arose about human performance way back in the early 20th century and this was put forward by two psychologists, Yerkes and Dodson. It is often called the 'inverted U' curve. In simple terms it suggests that we all need a certain amount of pressure if we are to perform well. Too little pressure and we can become bored eventually leading to a psychological state called 'rust-out'; too much pressure and we can panic and end up in the psychological state called 'burn-out'. It is the central zone where optimum performance lies and this is frequently termed the 'motivated well-being state'. We feel good about what we are doing, our brain is working well and we are producing the positive biochemistry of success with serotonin being produced and other beneficial responses from our psychological, physiological and neurological systems. In some cases this can be so powerful that we enter the 'flow' state, which we will discuss later in this chapter.

The relationship between pressure and performance:
the pressure/performance curve

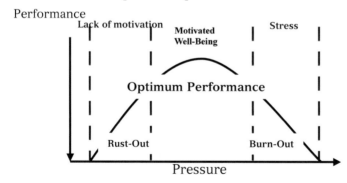

Working in the central zone of motivated well-being

This idea is of a central zone where we have enough but not too much pressure to reach optimal performance. We need some pressure to get us to swing into action, but not so much that we experience stress and even distress. One very useful tool to find out how much time you spend in the motivated well-being zone of optimum performance is the book The C Zone by Robert and Marilyn Kriegel, shown in the Resources section. The C Zone provides a questionnaire so that you can work out the proportion of the time you spend being under-motivated in the Drone Zone or over-motivated in the Panic Zone. A third score gives you an indication of how much time you are spending in the central C Zone of motivated well-being. It also gives you an insight into how your C Zone score has arisen and the actions you can take to spend more time there and less in the Panic and Drone Zones.

The Kriegels suggest that the C Zone score is made up from three areas:

- Commitment to a set of goals

- Confidence in our ability to perform our tasks

- The amount of control we have over our workload

It is interesting to relate these to purpose, mastery and autonomy which we have already discussed. When you analyse the C Zone scores, you identify which of these three factors score lower than the others and then put effort into that area. We all need the occasional high-pressure stimulus and the occasional low-pressure chill-out time, and this C Zone concept helps you gain that balance. It can also reduce the level of stress and pressure under which you are operating by giving you focus and a sense of satisfaction in a job well done. By reducing stress symptoms, your health and well-being will improve which is exactly what the central section is all about.

The roots of understanding performance – managing the inner game

Harnessing pressure effectively is a key issue in developing peak personal performance. Our thinking tends to control our lives whether we are consciously aware of it doing so or whether that control is on an unconscious level. One person who has written very useful material on the idea of managing the inner game is Timothy Gallwey in his *Inner Game* series. One of his core ideas is that in whatever we do – whether it is work, playing a sport, or performing with a musical instrument – we play two games. The outer game is our interacting with the context in which we are performing; the inner game is played in the arena of our mind. This leads us to the idea that whilst we might have a high level of potential performance in the outer game, the inner game being played often interferes with our ability to tap into our potential. Gallwey suggests a formula which is well worth remembering:

$P = p - I$ where P = actual performance, p=potential performance and I = interference

This suggests that actual performance achieved is potential performance minus interference. The art of peak performing is therefore about reducing the interference as much as possible. In simple terms, it is about going with the flow of the situation and not trying too hard. By trying too hard we often put ourselves into the Panic Zone as detailed above, worrying about how we are doing and whether we will be successful and win.

Interference often shows up as a series of stress responses such as doubting your own ability, feeling you have not prepared well enough and that your colleagues or audience will not like how you are performing. As well as the psychological effects, we can also experience many of the physical stress responses such as loss of breath, dry mouth, increased heartbeat, sweaty hands and feeling sick.

The key to handling the interference issue is to remember the power of the Law of Attraction. If you start to experience signs of stress you are probably thinking about what may go wrong and, in doing so, are tending to bring about the situation you fear. Instead it is more productive to think of the occasion when you performed to your best ability. Relive that experience in your mind and let it become your focus. Picture in your mind what you saw in that experience. Hear the sounds you heard in terms of what was being said and any background sounds. Thirdly revisit the feelings you felt. Feelings of elation, of joy, of confidence, and of being in control because you were performing really well. In the world of sport and artistic performance this technique, call anchoring, is used by many peak performers. It comes from the world of neurolinguistic programming and was originally a process developed from a common-sense approach to performance. Today, neuroscience research supports the idea with hard scientific evidence about how our brains work.

What we mean by 'flow' – the optimum performance state

Peak performance in the optimum central zone is something that we all need to aim for where possible if we are to tap into our potential and achieve all that we want to achieve. The ideal part of the optimum performance area leads to a state which we call 'flow'. Flow is a psychological state where we are energised, fully immersed in the activity and gaining great pleasure from operating at a high level whilst not experiencing untoward anxiety about the activity. Some people call this 'in the groove', 'in tune', 'centred' or 'focused'. The main contributor to our knowledge on flow is Mihaly Csikszentmihalyi, whose comprehensive book on the optimal experience is a 'must read' for the serious student of flow state.

Flow has been called hyperfocus, where an individual becomes totally focused on an activity to the exclusion of everything else. Remembering our discussions on goal setting and the 'real estate' effect, this is not to be encouraged. The six factors of the beneficial flow state are:

- Focused concentration on the activity of the moment

- A loss of reflective self-consciousness

- A blending of awareness and action

- A strong sense of control over the activity

- A temporary distortion or loss of awareness of time

- A feeling that the activity is intrinsically rewarding

To achieve a flow state, three conditions seem to need to be involved:

- The activity must have a clear set of goals and evidence of progress

- There must be feedback to enable the individual to adjust their behaviour to stay in the flow state

- There needs to be a good balance between the perceived challenge of the situation and the individual's perceived ability to perform the task

Put into simpler language, it is about:

- Knowing what to do

- Knowing how to do it

- Knowing how well you are performing

- Knowing where to go next in the process

- High-perceived challenges

- High-perceived skills

- Freedom from distractions

There are many applications for the flow state and the work situation is an area which concerns many people. Csikszentmihalyi suggests that to achieve flow in our work, we need three conditions to be met:

- The goals must be clear

- We need immediate feedback

- There needs to be a balance between opportunity and capacity

If we can learn to move ourselves into the flow state at will, then we will experience many benefits. We will feel good about ourselves, which will result in higher quality work. We will grow as people by developing self-mastery. Above all, we will make progress on our own personal journey by developing our ability to handle situations of increasing challenge.

Personal Kaizen – 1000 things, 1% better

Being a peak performer is not always about just the big-picture issues. It is also about what you do on a daily basis. In Japanese business culture, there is a total quality approach called Kaizen which is about making small improvements wherever you see an opportunity. This approach has been updated in many ways, one of which is the Will It Make The Boat Go Faster? technique in the book of the same name by Ben Hunt-Davis and Harriet Beveridge. This is a really interesting account of the reasons behind the success of the British Rowing Team in the 2000 Sydney Olympics. The text focuses on the idea that everyone in the team needs to focus on the goal and suggest ideas on how to make things better. What is clear from the Olympic experience is that keeping up the motivation is vital. The UK team had eight strategies for doing so:

- Believe in what you are doing and that success is possible

- Make the journey entertaining

- Get competitive

- Make yourself hungry for success

- Daydream

- Switch on your effort when it is needed

- Create measurable milestones and rewards

- Tackle big tasks with 10-minute spurts of effort

These ideas are all relevant to your success whether as an employee or running your own business. The importance of goals, of positive beliefs and action is heavily reinforced in this book, which is a significant contribution to thinking on success in whatever field it is applied.

Another excellent book on this subject of incremental perform-ance improvement is *The Slight Edge* by Jeff Olson. Olson argues that small changes made on a daily basis add up to big benefits. Those changes may include small differences in the way we undertake our work, increased exercise and dietary changes and a host of minor adjustments we can make to our lifestyle. Just think of five things you could do differently on a day-to-day basis that would give you great performance bene-fits.

Some Slight Edge examples

- Clear your emails each day to reduce your sense of elec-tronic overload

- Take 30 minutes' exercise each day to gain more energy

- Read something inspirational every day

- Play an educational CD in your car instead of listening to music

- Have one smaller meal a day which is low fat, low sugar and low salt

Taking the overview of your purpose and performance

In working out our sense of purpose it is useful to create a graphical representation of what we are all about. A useful tool for achieving this is the Ishikawa or fishbone diagram often used in problem solving. In this instance we are going to think about what it would take to be truly successful in the activity or business you are undertaking.

The starting point for creating the chart is to make a time log for 5 continuous days prior to setting up your chart. Record exactly what you spend your time doing, preferably in 15 minutes chunks. You will see that inevitably you encounter a number of time wasters. We need to eradicate these or at least manage and reduce them if we are to become a real peak performer.

The first issue to be decided is your purpose. What is your 'mission' and what is the main objective you want to achieve? You then consider the various issues and activities you will have to consider to bring that purpose to life and achieve the goal. Try to sort those areas into no more than seven branches, as research has shown that the conscious mind has difficulty holding more than seven (plus or minus two) ideas. You will undoubtedly think up other issues as you go along. However, for the present, let us say you want to be a successful IT consultant. Your fishbone diagram might look like the one below. This is not to say that it is necessarily the right way to be a top-line IT consultant; it is simply one person's approach, showing how they want to proceed with a sense of purpose.

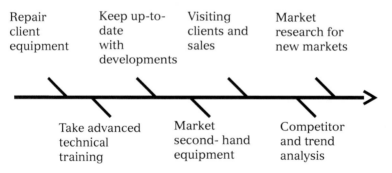

| Repair client equipment | Keep up-to-date with developments | Visiting clients and sales | Market research for new markets |

| Take advanced technical training | Market second- hand equipment | Competitor and trend analysis |

We then decide how much time each week we intend to spend working on our plan. Let's say it is 40 hours. With seven branches, that is just under six hours per week. It is almost certain that we will not spend an equal amount of time on each of the seven areas. The best way to proceed is to divide up your 'time cake' so that you choose, say, three hours on area one, six hours on area two, four hours on area three and so on until you have allocated your full 40 hours. Invariably you will not stick rigidly to these times. Some weeks you will spend more than the allocated time on one or more area, less on others. However, it does give you a plan and a benchmark to proceed and build in overall balance.

The big issue that now arises for many people is the case where the time needed to accomplish all the work vastly exceeds the time we have allocated. In this situation we need to work with priorities.

Working with priorities

The Pareto principle

We can easily get drawn into the activity trap and be very busy without achieving the results for which we are aiming. We have to prioritise and there are several ways to do this. Firstly it is important to be aware of the 80/20 rule suggested by management consultant Joseph Juran who named it after the Italian economist Vilfredo Pareto. He observed that 80% of the land in Italy was owned by 20% of the people and also that 20% of the pea pods in his garden contained 80% of the peas. He surmised that perhaps there was a general law here and that seems to be true. A common rule of thumb in business is that 20% of your sales come from 80% of your clients and 80% of your sales from 20% of your clients. Many natural phenomena follow the Pareto distribution and so it seems worth giving some consideration to its application in time management.

So for each of your branches in the fishbone diagram, work out the 20% of activities which will bring 80% of the value and then focus on that 20%. You may be able to delegate much of the other 80%, postpone it until it becomes high value and maybe not even engage in it. By working on the high value 20%, you will be doing 80% of what is possible, and over the full range of your activity, that will give you excellent performance outcomes. Remember to work on the top 20% in all your seven branches and try not to do 100% in any one branch unless there are very special circumstances.

The urgency importance matrix

This has been covered by many writers including Stephen Covey in his great book *The 7 Habits of Highly Effective People*. Covey suggests that we consider all the tasks we have to under-take in terms of their urgency and their importance. They are then placed on the grid as below:

	Urgent	Not urgent
Important		
Not important		

By focusing on the urgent and important, we fine tune our efforts for maximum output. We can then focus on the important and not urgent and fit in the not important tasks as and when we feel the time is right.

The to-do list and schedule

Many people just make a list of what they have to do and, as a result, they often do not apply this tool effectively. I first make a master list of everything I have to do but then I park that list and I do not worry about how large it is or whether I will achieve everything. I look at the master list and then code everything either A, B or C. 'A' items are of high importance and urgent and must be done, 'B' are important and should be done as soon as time is available, and the 'C' items can wait until they can be fitted into you plan. I divide my master list into two sections: the things I will focus on and the things that the universe will take care of. This last idea may seem somewhat strange. However, there is a point to it. Firstly, it is important to log somewhere all the tasks we have to accomplish but, at the same time, not cause ourselves to be anxious about whether we are going to accomplish them. By saying the universe will take care of them, we are actually asking our unconscious to keep them on the radar until we can get around to their completion. What you will find with the to-do list approach is that as you become more productive your master list will shrink and you will eventually get around to completing all the tasks and making way for new tasks which arise.

One key aspect of this tool is scheduling. We often have tasks which need our full attention and which may take an hour or more to accomplish. In this case, schedule a time period to devote to the task uninterrupted. Treat it with the same reverence you would a meeting with your manager or important client. In that way you will ramp up your productivity and the quality of the work. A really large task may require several scheduled periods. In my writing work I find that a two-hour slot is the optimum. More than that period of time and I start to find the going tough; if I devote less than two hours, I don't seem to find the sustained focus I need to put together the ideas.

Value-based time management

This is a very important concept for the self-employed and the business owner. Work out what your time is worth when you look at the income from your business efforts and subtract the expenses and costs. You are not left with profit because you have not yet paid yourself. Let's say you decide to pay yourself £20.00 per hour. That is a good income for a 40-hour week. Look at the work you complete each day and the hours involved. Has the outcome been worth £20.00 per hour or could you have outsourced that piece of work for, say, £12.00 per hour and used your time more effectively somewhere else? We all need to gain a sound awareness of the value issue if we are to run our business lives effectively.

The Personal Performance Planner concept

This idea came from combining the ideas of many time management experts and I have adapted it to work for my particular situation. Notice we write a summary of our goals to keep us on track.

PERSONAL PERFORMANCE PLANNER

Date

Goals for this week	Daily goal activity

The top things to do today	Things the universe will take care of

Schedule	Activity	Contacts phone and e-mail

Physical activity	Relaxation	Reflection

I then put the full master list on the sheet, dividing it into those things which need urgent attention today and those things which are in the frame for effort later down the line. There are spaces for scheduling work and then phone calls and contacts which need to be made. Finally, and most important, I programme three special times: some physical activity to keep up the energy, some relaxation to balance that effort, and some time out to just think and reflect on everything that is going on. This tool is immensely powerful in creating focus whilst building in focused effort and the opportunity to visit several flow states throughout the day.

Summary

In this chapter we have looked at what it means to be a peak performer and some ideas for working towards that end. We identified, through the work of Charles Garfield, the six characteristics of peak performers including a compelling sense of mission and purpose, creating outstanding results in real time, and gaining self-mastery and effective self-management. Collaboration skills, making appropriate course corrections and managing change effectively were also identified. You were then given the opportunity to reflect on the extent to which you might qualify as a peak performer.

The human performance curve was introduced and this led to the C-Zone concept where we aim to spend most our time in the motivated well-being state and less time in the rust-out or burn-out areas. Three key issues to ensure we spend as much time as possible in the C Zone were identified: commitment to a set of goals, confidence in our ability to perform our tasks to a high standard, and increasing the amount of control we feel we have over our work.

The inner game concept of Timothy Gallwey was presented with the idea that actual performance is potential performance minus the impact of interference, that little voice in your head that is critical of your efforts and creates anxiety. The 'flow' state was then described and the conditions to create flow presented.

Specific tools to aid peak personal performance were then given including Kaizen, Will It Make the Boat Go Faster? and the Slight Edge. The Ishikawa or fishbone diagram was then discussed, which enables you to take a strategic overview of your work and assign priorities. Methods including the Pareto principle, the urgency importance matrix, to-do lists and schedules were covered.

A method for daily personal performance planning was presented.

Development questions

- In which areas of your work do you have the potential to become a peak performer?

- What percentage of your work time do you spend in each of the three zones of rust-out, motivated well-being and burn-out? (You might like to check this with the on-line C-Zone questionnaire or with the hard copy questionnaire in the book.)

- Think of three major areas where you have to perform tasks. For each area, consider how potential performance is reduced by interference. What steps can you take to reduce the impact of that interference?

- What flow states have you experienced at work?

- In what areas of your life would you like to experience a flow state and how will you set about enabling this to happen?

- Can you identify a list of 20 ideas on how you can become more like a peak performer in the work you undertake?

- Can you name six Slight Edge changes that you can make to move you more into the motivated well-being peak performer state?

- Have you created your Ishikawa fishbone diagram to create a strategic overview of the work you do and how you will undertake it in future?

- How well do you prioritise your work? Can you apply at least two prioritising methods to your work?

- Have you prepared a Personal Performance Planner sheet for at least five consecutive days?

Now please rate your understanding and application of the material in Chapter Eleven and complete mini circle 11 on the dashboard overleaf. Update your progress on the material of the earlier chapters in preparation for creating your strategic action plan.

Progress review dashboard

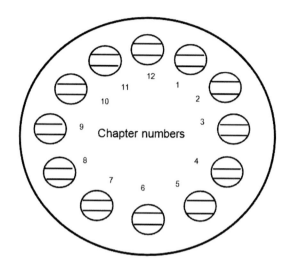

Chapter numbers

I understand most of the ideas in this chapter and intend applying those which appeal to me

I fully understand the ideas in this chapter and having made some progress in applying them

I am fully committed to applying the ideas in this chapter and have made great progress and I am moving forwards with achieving my goals as I set new ones

Chapter Twelve
Taking action and creating your strategic plan

"Be the change that you wish to see in the world – the future depends on what you do today." **Mahatma Gandhi**

A reminder: **knowledge on its own is not power,** it is the application of knowledge and learning from results which puts you in a powerful position. In this chapter, we are going to identify how to create your strategic and operational activity to bring your vision into reality.

To set the scene I want you to make a contract with yourself to work diligently on putting the contents of this book to work for you whether you are in your own business, an employee or just starting out in the world of work. Let us start with the big-picture issues.

- What is your vision for the future that you would like to experience?

- What is your purpose in life and the mission you will undertake to bring your vision into reality?

- What is important to you about the way you go about achieving your vision?

- What are the seven key underpinning values that are important to you?

How would you describe your present position in terms of the EPISTLE factors of your economic situation, the political frame, information your have and need, social trends, technological aspects, legal considerations and environmental issues?

Using Chapter Three on Setting Direction, start to give some thought to the goals you wish to reach in the following areas:

- Family

- Relationships

- Career and business

- Financial

- Educational

- Health and physical fitness

- Leisure

- Community

- Personal

Choose a spread of goals over as many of these areas as possible, both tangible and intangible. Then start thinking about long-term, medium-term and short-term goals.

What are your long-term goals for at least three years in the future?

What are your medium-term goals for the next year?

What are your short-term goals for next month?

Taking the more detailed aspects of the book, what do you believe are the positive beliefs you have about yourself and your ability?

What are some of the less positive beliefs you have about yourself and your ability?

What action will you take to build on your positive belief set?

Carry out a TPN analysis based on the ideas in Chapter Four so that you can identify the problems over which you have control and can take action.

Review your financial and commercial awareness skills and gain some basic knowledge of finance and accountancy using the sources mentioned in Chapter Five.

Think about your networking skills and the people it would be beneficial for you to contact and with whom you should build working relationships.

Read at least one of the books on selling skills and one on negotiation skills.

Create your own personal leadership development programme using the ideas in Chapter Nine.

Start crafting your own personal strategic plan using the ideas in Chapter Ten.

Review the material on peak performance in Chapter Eleven and develop your work-life balance skills, with time for relaxation and reflection to enable you to develop insights on your major issues.

You might like to copy the next page and complete the sections so that you can pin it up above your desk to keep you on track! Please feel free to copy it again so that you can update it as you move forwards.

My Personal Commitment Contract to bring my vision into reality

Name...

My personal vision is...

....

....

My elevator pitch is..

....

....

....

I will regularly use my vision board to recharge my motivation by adding new items and adjusting my priorities

My core values are

....

....

....

....

....

....

....

I will carry out my work to the best of my ability, focus on what I want to achieve, develop high-quality working relationships and enjoy life to the full

Signed..

Date..

Now rate your understanding and application of the strategic template shown in this chapter and complete mini circle 12 on the dashboard overleaf. Take this time to review your performance on all the chapters in the book.

Choose the areas in the book which interest you the most and which will help in your development. Start researching the relevant books, internet links and DVE programmes in the Resources section.

Progress review dashboard

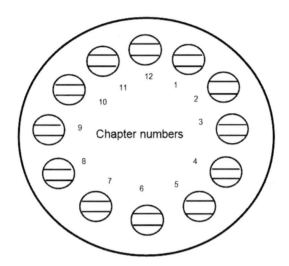

Chapter numbers

 I understand most of the ideas in this chapter and intend applying those which appeal to me

 I fully understand the ideas in this chapter and having made some progress in applying them

 I am fully committed to applying the ideas in this chapter and have made great progress and I am moving forwards with achieving my goals as I set new ones

Resources and further reading

Chapter One

Rohn, J (1996) *7 Strategies for Wealth and Happiness* Three Rivers Press, New York

Rock, D (2007) *Quiet Leadership* HarperCollins

Ziglar, Z (2012) *Born to Win* AudioInk

Byrne, R (2006) *The Secret* Atria books, Beyond Words Publishing

Byrne, R (2012) *The Magic* Simon & Schuster

Wattles, W D (rev 2007) *The Science of Getting Rich* LifeSuccess Productions

Hill, N (1937,1966) *Think and Grow Rich* Wilshire Book Company, N Hollywood

Nightingale, E (2007) *Lead the Field* Beta Nu Publishing

Nightingale, E (2013) *The Strangest Secret* Merchant Books

Proctor, R (1997) *You Were Born Rich* LifeSuccess Productions

Chapter Two

Rohn, J (1996) *7 Strategies for Wealth and Happiness* Three Rivers Press, New York

Rock, D (2007) *Quiet Leadership* HarperCollins

Pink, D (2011) *Drive* Canongate Books

Rogers, C R (1989) *A Therapist's View of Psychotherapy* Constable

Kroeger, O & Thusen, J M (reissue 1989) *Type Talk* Dell

Rogers, C R (1989) A Therapist's View of Psychotherapy Constable

Kroeger, O & Thusen, J M (reissue 1989) Type Talk Dell

Maltz, M (1960), *Psycho-cybernetics*, Melvin Powers, Wilshire Book Company, Hollywood, USA

Chapter Three

Hooper, A & Potter, J (1997) The Business of Leadership Gower Ashgate

Assaraf, J & Smith, M (2008) The Answer Simon & Schuster

Assaraf, J (2007) You Can Have It All Simon & Schuster

Tracy, B (2nd edition 2010) Goals Berrett-Koehler

Mayne, B (2006) Goal Mapping Watkins Publishing

Chapter Four

Allison, M (1993) *The Problem Buster's Guide* Gower

Nightingale, E (2007) *Lead the Field* Beta Nu Publishing

Grint, K (2007) *Leadership, Management and Command: Rethinking D-Day* Palgrave Macmillan

Hooper, A & Potter, J (2001) *Intelligent Leadership* Random House

Brown, M (1994) *The Dinosaur Strain* Innovation Centre Europe

Nolan, V (1989) *The Innovator's Handbook* Sphere Books

West, M A (1997) *Developing Creativity in Organisations,* British Psychological Society

Von Oech, R (1992) *A Whack on the Side of the Head* Creative Think, Menlo Park

Chapter Five

Clason, G S (1955) *The Richest Man in Babylon,* Hawthorn / Dutton, New York

Byrne, R (2006) *The Secret* Atria books, Beyond Words Publishing

Kyiosaki, R (2nd edition, 2011) *Rich Dad Poor Dad* Plata Publishing

Boyce, T & Lake, C (2007) *The Commercial Manager* Thorogood

Mason, R (2012) *Finance for Non-Financial Managers* Hodder Education

Chapter Six

Royal, M & Agnew, T (2011) *The Enemy of Engagement* AMACOM

Rock, D (2007) *Quiet Leadership* HarperCollins

LeBoeuf, M (1989) *How to Win Customers and Keep Them for Life* Berkley Books

Dunar, M (2013) *Rapport: Easily Double Your Rapport Skills Within One Week* Fluency books on Amazon

Timperley, J (2002) *Network Success* Piatkus Books, London

Rich, D A (2004) *How to Click with Everyone Every Time* McGraw Hill

Chapter Seven

Laborde, G Z (1987) *Influencing with Integrity* Syntony Publishing, Palo Alto, California

Carnegie, D (1976) *How to Win Friends and Influence People* Cedar Books, Worlds Work Ltd

Littauer, F (2007) *Personality Plus* Monach Books

Cialdini, R B (2009) *Influence Science and Practice* Pearson Education

Borg, J (2009) *Persuasion – The Art of Influencing People* Pearson Education

Miller, R B & Williams, G A (2004) *The Five Paths to Persuasion* Warner Business Books, New York

Vickers, A, Bavister, S & Smith, J (2009) *Personal Impact* Pearson Education

Isaacs, W (1999) *Dialogue and the Art of Thinking Together* Random House

Stone, D, Patton, B & Heen, S (2000) *Difficult Conversations* Penguin Books

Harvard Business Essentials various authors (2005) *Power, Influence and Persuasion* Harvard Business School

Conger, J, (May 1998) *The Necessary Art of Persuasion*, Harvard Business Review, Harvard Business School

Miller, R B & Williams, G A (2002) *Change the Way you Persuade* Harvard Business Review, Harvard Business School

Chapter Eight

Ziglar, Z (2012) *Born to Win* AudioInk

Pink, D (2012) *To Sell is Human* Canongate, London

Morgen, S D (1993) *Sales on the Line* Metamorphosis Press, Portland

Burg, B (2006) *Endless Referrals* McGraw Hill

Johnson, K L (2010) *Selling with NLP* Nicholas Brealey, London

O'Brien, J (2013) *Negotiation for Purchasing Professionals* Kogan Page

Karrass, C L (1996) *In Business as in Life – You Don't Get What You Deserve, You Get What You Negotiate* Stanford St Press, Beverly Hills

Harvard Business Essentials various authors (2003) *Negotiation* Harvard Business School

Brian Tracy's 24 Effective Closing Techniques

http://www.briantracy.com/freegifts/24effectiveclosingtechniquesup.pdf

Richard Fenton and Andrea Waltz

http://www.goforno.com

Chapter Nine

Hooper, A & Potter, J (1997) *The Business of Leadership* Gower Ashgate

Hooper, A & Potter, J (2001) *Intelligent Leadership* Random House

Daft, R L (2011) *Leadership* South Western Cengage Learning

Adair, J (1983) *Effective Leadership* Gower

Goleman, D l (2002) *The New Leaders* Sphere Books

Hooper, A (ed 2006) *Leadership Perspectives* Ashgate

Kouzes, J M & Posner, B Z (1995) *The Leadership Challenge* Jossey-Bass

Rath,T & Conchie, B (2008) *Strengths Based Leadership* Gallup Press

Yemm, G (2013) *Leading your Team* Financial Times Publishing

Goleman, D. (March-April 2000) *Leadership That Gets Results,* Harvard Business Review, Harvard Business School

Chapter Ten

W Chan Kim & Mauborgne, R (2005) *Blue Ocean Strategy* Harvard Business Review Press

Grundy, T (2004) *Gurus on Business Strategy* Thorogood

Harvard Business Essentials various authors (2005) *Strategy* Harvard Business School

Witcher, J & Chau, V S (2010) *Strategic Management Principles and Practice* South Western Cengage Learning

Assaraf, J & Smith, M (2008) *The Answer* Atria Books, Simon & Schuster

Chapter Eleven

Garfield, C (1986) *Peak Performers* Avon Books, New York

Kriegel, R & Kriegel, M H (1985) *Peak Performance Under Pressure – The C Zone* Cedar Books, Heinemann

Csikszentmihalyi, M & Csikszentmihalyi, I S (1995) *Optimal Experience – Psychological Studies of Flow in Consciousness* Cambridge University Press

Gallwey, W (2001) *The Inner Game of Work* Random House

Covey, S R (1989) *The 7 Habits of Highly Effective People* Simon & Schuster

Gleeson, K (2000) *The Personal Efficiency Program* John Wiley & Sons

Hunt-Davis, B & Beveridge, H (2011) *Will It Make The Boat Go Faster?* Matador, Troubador Publishing Ltd, Leicester

Olson, J (2011) *The Slight Edge* Success Books, Lake Dallas, Texas

Charlesworth, E A & Nathan, R G (1987) *Stress Management* Corgi Books

Adair, J (1987) *How to Manage Your Time* Talbot Adair

Mackenzie, R A (1972) *The Time Trap* AMACOM McGraw-Hill

Audio and DVE programmes available from Nightingale Conant, Torquay, Devon, UK

Lead the Field Earl Nightingale

The Strangest Secret Earl Nightingale

The Science of Getting Rich Bob Proctor

The Secret Rhonda Byrne (also available www.thesecret.tv)

Action Strategies for Personal Achievement Brian Tracy

The 7 Habits of Highly Effective People Stephen Covey

The Born to Win Seminar Zig Ziglar

There are many more titles in the Nightingale Conant brochure.